PONS

H0331049

Gewusst wie!

Grammatik-Training
ENGLISCH 5. Klasse

Wer`s versteht, lernt leichter.

von
Julia Grieß

Ernst Klett Sprachen GmbH
Barcelona • Belgrad • Budapest • Ljubljana • London • Posen
Prag • Sofia • Stuttgart • Zagreb

PONS
Gewusst wie!
Grammatik-Training
ENGLISCH 5. Klasse

Wer`s versteht, lernt leichter.

von
Julia Grieß

Auflage A1 5 4 3 2 1 / 2010 2009 2008 2007

Internet: www.pons.de
E-Mail: info@pons.de

Redaktion: Birgit Piefke-Wagner, Debby Rebsch
Logoentwurf: Erwin Poell, Heidelberg
Logoüberarbeitung: Sabine Redlin, Ludwigsburg
Illustrationen: Stefan Theurer
Einbandgestaltung: Schmidt & Dupont
Titelfoto: Vlado Golub, Stuttgart
Layout/Satz: andrea grundmann kommunikationsgestaltung, Karlsruhe
Druck: Legoprint
Printed in Italy.
ISBN: 978-3-12-561382-9

Herzlich Willkommen!

Mit dem **PONS Gewusst wie! Grammatik-Training** hast du ein Übungsbuch, mit dem du gezielt bestimmte grammatische Themen wiederholen und üben kannst.

Wie ist das Buch aufgebaut?

Wir haben verschiedene grammatische Themen zu einem Themenblock zusammengefasst. Jeder Themenblock endet mit einem Test. Die **Kapitel** gehen meistens über zwei Seiten (manchmal auch über vier) und sind so aufgebaut, dass du auf der ersten (rechten) Seite die Erklärung zu einem Thema erarbeitest. Dann blätterst du um und wendest die Regeln zu diesem Thema in verschiedenen Übungen an, ohne die Erklärung zu sehen.
Im **Test** kannst du überprüfen, wie gut du die vorhergehenden Themen beherrschst. Im Anhang findest du die **Lösungen**, die **Wortliste**, in der du die wichtigsten englischen Wörter nachschlagen kannst, und eine Tabelle mit den **unregelmäßigen Verben**.

Dieses Symbol bedeutet ‚Achtung!' und weist dich auf Ausnahmen oder knifflige Sonderregeln hin. Diese Informationen sind besonders wichtig.

Hier findest du entweder einen Tipp zur Lösung der Übung oder einen weiterführenden Lerntipp.

Nicht alle grammatischen Themen, die hier behandelt werden, stehen in jedem Bundesland oder in jeder Schulart auch auf dem Lehrplan. Diese Themen oder Übungen haben wir mit einem Sternchen markiert.

Wie arbeitest du sinnvoll mit dem Buch?

Du kannst mit der **Bestandsaufnahme** beginnen, um auf die Schnelle zu sehen, welche Themen du noch üben solltest. Die Lösungen sagen dir, in welchem Kapitel das Thema bearbeitet wird. Oder du machst die Bestandsaufnahme am Schluss, um deine Fortschritte zu sehen.
Wenn du schon weißt, wo du mehr Übung brauchst, suchst du dir im **Inhaltsverzeichnis** gezielt Kapitel aus. Natürlich kannst du die Themen auch in der vorgegebenen Reihenfolge durcharbeiten.
Bei den Sternchenthemen und -übungen solltest du in deinem Schulbuch nachschauen, ob sie in diesem Schuljahr behandelt werden. Wenn ja, dann solltest du sie auf jeden Fall bearbeiten. Wenn sie für dich kein Thema sind, kannst du es trotzdem versuchen oder bis zum nächsten Schuljahr warten. Überspringe dann in den Tests die Sternchenübungen.

Viel Spaß und Erfolg beim Lernen!

Inhaltsverzeichnis

I

Inhaltsverzeichnis

Bestandsaufnahme

1 Welche Form von to be gehört in die Lücke?
a) Jason ____ a nice boy. ○ *is* ○ *are* ○ *am*
b) We ____ in class 5. ○ *is* ○ *are* ○ *am*

2 Wie lautet eine Frage mit to be?
○ a) Have you got a dog? ○ b) Are you from England? ○ c) Do you like rock music?

3 Wie lautet die Frage zur Antwort:
My name is Sally.
○ a) Where are you from? ○ b) How old are you? ○ c) What's your name?

4 Wie lautet ein Satz in der Verneinung mit to be?
○ a) I don't like school. ○ b) Peter isn't reading a book. ○ c) Helen is at my school.

5 Welche Form des Verbs gehört in die Lücke?
1. Kim often ____ (*visit*) her aunt Helen in London.
○ a) *is visiting* ○ b) *visited* ○ c) *visits*
2. Jason ____ (*not play*) baseball on Mondays.
○ a) *isn't playing* ○ b) *doesn't play*
○ c) *didn't play*
3. Jim and John ____ (*go*) swimming every Tuesday afternoon. ○ a) *aren't going*
○ b) *are going* ○ c) *go*

6 In welcher Zeit steht die folgende Frage?
Do you like Geography?
○ a) simple present
○ b) present progressive
○ c) simple past

7 Wie lautet die Kurzantwort auf die folgenden Fragen?
1. Do Peter and John always write English tests on Mondays?
○ a) Yes, he does. ○ b) Yes, they did.
○ c) No, they don't.
2. Does Sarah often read funny books?
○ a) No, she didn't. ○ b) Yes, he does.
○ c) Yes, she does.

8 Welcher Satz steht im present progressive?
○ a) Gerry likes ice cream.
○ b) Jason and Jo are doing their homework.
○ c) Tom went to school by bus.

9 Wie lautet die Frage zur Antwort: He is eating a piece of pizza.
○ a) Do you eat a pizza? ○ b) Are you eating a pizza? ○ c) What is he doing at the moment?

10 Welcher Satz steht in der Verneinung des present progressive?
○ a) Jane doesn't like comics.
○ b) Jane didn't like the new book.
○ c) Jane isn't reading a book.

11 Wie lauten die Antworten auf die folgenden Fragen?
1. Where do you live?
○ a) I live in Berlin.
○ b) I'm living in Berlin.
○ c) I lived in Berlin.
2. Who is your best friend?
○ a) Tom was my best friend.
○ b) Jane is my best friend.

B

12 Lies den Text und die zwei Fragen. Entscheide, welche Antwort richtig ist.

It's 8.15 on Monday morning. Helen is late for school. She hasn't got much time left. Yesterday she was late, too. Her teacher was very angry. She doesn't want to knock at the door. She's afraid.

1. What time is it? a) It's quarter past nine. b) It's quarter past eight. c) It's quarter past ten.
2. Who was angry yesterday? a) Her mum was angry. b) Her teacher is angry. c) Her teacher was angry.

13 Welches Wort gehört in die Lücken?
1. There is ___ lemonade in the bottle. a) *much* b) *many* c) *a lot of*
2. How ___ pupils are in your class? a) *much* b) *many* c) *a lot of*

14 Wie lautet die Übersetzung der Präposition in den folgenden Sätzen?
1. The dog is **behind** the house. a) neben b) vor c) auf d) hinter
2. Jim and Tim are playing **in front of** the house. a) vor b) hinter c) neben d) unter

15 Finde passende Übersetzungen für die unterstrichenen Satzteile.
1. Jemand sagt, dass er <u>die Jacke hier</u> sehr schön findet. a) this jacket here b) that jacket over there c) these jackets here
2. John und Jim sagen, dass sie <u>die neuen CDs da drüben</u> schon kennen. a) those new CDs over there b) these new CDs here c) that new CD over there

16 Kreuze das richtige Verbindungswort an: and, or, but oder so.
Last year I went to Australia *and* *or* *but* *so* I visited my uncle Sam.
My uncle was very happy to see me, *and* *or* *but* *so* his dog wasn't happy.
My aunt had dinner ready when we came home, *and* *or* *but* *so* we sat down *and* *or* *but* *so* had dinner.

17 Wie lautet die Übersetzung?
1. Der Freund meiner Schwester
a) The boyfriends' sister b) My sister's boyfriend c) My sisters' boyfriend
2. Der Name der Straße
a) The street's name b) The street of the name c) The name of the street

18 Welche Uhrzeit wird angezeigt?
1. 4:30 a) It's quarter past four. b) It's half past five. c) It's half past four.
2. 7:45 a) It's quarter past seven. b) It's quarter to eight. c) It's half past seven.

19 Welcher Possessivbegleiter passt hier?
This is Jane's bag. It's ___ bag. a) *his* b) *their* c) *her* c) *me*

Grammatikbegriffe

adjective	Adjektiv, Wie-wort (careful)
adverb	Adverb (carefully)
adverbial of place / time	Adverbiale Bestimmung des Ortes / der Zeit
article, definite / indefinite	Artikel, bestimmter / unbestimmter (the / a,an)
auxiliary	Hilfsverb (be, do, have)
conjunction / connective	Konjunktion, Bindewort (and, but, if, because, etc.)
consonant	Konsonant, Mitlaut (b, t, k, l, p, s, t, etc.)
s-genitive	s-Genitiv (my sister's friend)
of-genitive	of-Genitiv (the title of the book)
imperative	Imperativ, Befehlsform
infinitive	Infinitiv, Grundform (1. Form)
long form	Langform
modal	Modales Hilfsverb (can, must, mustn't, needn't)
noun	Substantiv, Nomen
negative form	Verneinung
number	Zahl
cardinal numbers	Grundzahlen (1, 5, 12, 465, 1,000, etc.)
ordinal numbers	Ordnungszahlen (1st, 2nd, 3rd, 4th, etc.)
object	Objekt (Wen oder was? Wem?)
plural	Plural, Mehrzahl
possessive determiner	Possessivbegleiter, Besitzanzeigendes Fürwort
preposition	Präposition (in, on, under, next to, in front of, etc.)
present progressive	Verlaufsform der Gegenwart
pronoun	Pronomen, Fürwort
object pronoun	Personalpronomen im Objektfall (me, him, etc.)
personal pronoun	Personalpronomen (I, you, he, she, it, we, you, they)
question	Frage
question word	Fragewort (what, where, who, when, why, how)
sentence	Satz
short answer	Kurzantwort (Yes, I am. No, I'm not.)
short form	Kurzform (I'm, he's, you aren't, we've, she hasn't)
simple past	einfache Vergangenheit
simple present	Präsens, einfache Gegenwart
singular	Singular, Einzahl
subject	Subjekt (Wer oder was?)
verb	Verb, Prädikat, Tunwort
regular verb	regelmäßiges Verb (play, answer, ask, etc.)
irregular verb	unregelmäßiges Verb (be, go, tell, write, run, etc.)
vowel	Vokal (a, e, i, o, u), Selbstlaut
word order	Wortstellung (S_V_O, Ort vor Zeit)

Formen von *to be*

1 Erste Unterhaltungen auf Englisch. Unterstreiche die Formen von to be im Text.

Jane: I'm eleven. Helen is my best friend.
Tony: I'm eleven, too. Taylor and Gerry are my best friends. They are eleven and twelve.
Helen: Hello, what's your name?
Iris: My name is Iris and this is Jack, my dog.

2 Schreibe die Frage mit to be aus dem Text oben auf:

____

3 Hier sind weitere Fragen mit to be. Bringe sie in die richtige Reihenfolge.

1. is | Mrs White | your | teacher ______________________________ ?
2. they | are | your | in | class ______________________________ ?
3. where | you | are | from ______________________________ ?
4. is | who | in | my | room ______________________________ ?

Nach den Fragewörtern wie who, where *oder* what steht immer direkt eine Form von to be.

4 Ordne den Fragen die richtigen Antworten zu.

1. Is this your book?
2. Are they new here?
3. How are you?
4. Is Tom new here?

a) I'm fine, thank you.
b) Yes, he is.
c) Yes, they are.
d) No, it isn't.

5 Verneinung von to be.

Die Kurzform von I am not heißt immer I'm not!

1. Susan isn't eleven. She's ten.
2. No, I'm not from Glasgow.
3. They aren't in my class.
4. Peter and John aren't from London. They're from Cardiff.

Die Verneinung von to be kann isn't (is not), I'm not (I am not) oder aren't (are not) lauten.

Formen von *to be*

6 Setze am, is oder are in die Lücken ein.

1. He ______ in my class.
2. Jenny and Zoe ______ good friends.
3. Tommy ______ a good football player.
4. They ______ eleven years old.
5. The cat ______ black.
6. I ______ from Cologne.

7 Beantworte die Fragen mit Kurzantworten.

1. Are you in year 5? ______
2. Are the boys in your class OK? ______
3. Is your school in France? ______
4. Is your English teacher nice? ______

★ 8 Formuliere die Fragen auf Englisch.

1. Frage Maria, ob sie zwölf Jahre alt ist. ______
2. Frage Mark, ob Tim aus England kommt. ______
3. Frage Julie, ob die Mädchen in der Schule sind. ______
4. Frage Mrs Thomson, ob sie deine neue Lehrerin ist. ______

9 Entscheide, welche Form man von to be braucht und schreibe die Sätze dann richtig auf.

1. <u>not to be</u> | Jack | best | friend | my *Jack isn't my best friend.*
2. he | <u>not to be</u> | my | in | class ______
3. Zoe | <u>to be</u> | London | from ______
4. tutor | <u>not to be</u> | my | Mr Old | school | at ______

★ 10 Wie lautet die Frage? Schreibe die Frage zur vorgegebenen Antwort auf.

1. ______? Yes, I'm new here.
2. ______? Helen is ten years old.

Personalpronomen

1 Welche Personalpronomen findest du in der Sprechblase?
Schreibe sie auf und ergänze die fehlenden Personalpronomen.

Singular: ____________________

Plural: ____________________

Notiere dir die Besonderheiten beim Personalpronomen you.
Das Personalpronomen you hat mehrere

____________________ .

Es kann ____________ , ____________ ,

____________ , Sie und Ihnen heißen.

2 Ordne nun die entsprechenden Formen von to be (am – are – is) den Personalpronomen zu.

Singular		Plural	
Langform	**Kurzform**	**Langform**	**Kurzform**
I am	*I'm*	*we* ________	________
you are	________	*you* ________	________
he ________	________	*they* ________	________
she ________	________		
it ________	________		

3 Billy the mouse und Kitty the cat treffen Candy the dog und stellen ein paar Fragen.

Billy:	Are you new here?	Yes, I am.	**Kitty:**	Are we friends now?	Yes, we are.
Billy:	Is he nice, Kitty?	Yes, he is.	**Candy:**	Are you two hungry, too?	No, we aren't.
Kitty:	Am I a cool cat?	Yes, you are.	**Candy:**	Is she your girlfriend?	Yes, she is.

Mit welchen Personalpronomen ist keine Frage gebildet? Mit ________ und ________ .

6 Denke dir eine eigene Frage zu den fehlenden Personalpronomen aus Übung 3 aus.

1. ____________________

2. ____________________

Personalpronomen

5 Füge die fehlenden Formen in den Brief ein: I – am- am- am – he – is- is – we – are- are.

Hello ____________________,
I ______ a star and I ______ twelve. Marvin ______ my friend. ______ is a star, too. He ______ from Germany. ______ are both from Germany. We ______ popstars. ______ you good at school? I ______ not good at school. But ______ am a star.
Love, Whitney ☺☺☺

6 Schreibe einen Brief zurück und erzähle über dich, deine Familie und deinen Freund / deine Freundin.

Hello Whitney,
I'm ________________________ and I'm ____________________. My friend is ____
____
Love, ________________________ ☺☺☺

7 Ersetze die unterstrichenen Satzteile durch ein Personalpronomen.

1. <u>Mrs Taylor</u> wants to meet <u>Jason</u>. ______________________
2. <u>The cat</u> sees <u>the mouse</u> in the garden. ______________________
3. <u>Jacky and Helen</u> like <u>Theresa</u>. ______________________

8 Welche der Fragen ist richtig? Die Buchstaben hinter den richtigen Fragen ergeben ein Wort.

1. a) He from London is? N
   b) German you are? O
   c) Is he from London? P

2. a) Are you German? E
   b) From London he is? R
   c) You German are? I

3. a) Am I your in class? U
   b) Am I in your class? T
   c) In your I am class? L

4. a) Is a good film it? W
   b) Is it a good film? S
   c) A good film it is? A

Lösungswort:

1.	2.	3.	4.

Personalpronomen als Objekt

1 Übersetze die unterstrichenen Personalpronomen im Akkusativ und im Dativ.

Akkusativ		Dativ		Nominativ	
Pete likes me.	mich	You can help me.	mir	I	ich
I like you.	____	I can help you.	____	you	du/Sie
We like him.	____	We can help him.	____	he	er
She likes her.	____	I can help her.	____	she	sie
They like it.	____	You can help it.	____	it	es
He likes us.	____	They can help us.	____	we	wir
We like you.	____	We can help you.	____	you	ihr/Sie
We like them.	____	They can help them.	____	they	sie

Im Englischen sind die Personalpronomen im Akkusativ und Dativ identisch, im Deutschen nicht!

2 Die Personalpronomen haben verschiedene Bedeutungen. Übersetze das unterstrichene Wort.

1. Let's meet him at 7 o'clock. ihn
2. She can see them. ____
3. I can give him the book. ____
4. We can give them the book. ____

3 Verschiedene Übersetzungen von it.

1. I can see the school. I can see it. Ich kann sie sehen.
2. I can see the table. I can see it. Ich kann ____ sehen.
3. I can see the book. I can see it. Ich kann ____ sehen.

It steht für Gegenstände in der Einzahl, ganz gleich, ob der Gegenstand im Deutschen weiblich, männlich oder sächlich ist.

Personalpronomen als Objekt

4 Setze die fehlenden Pronomen ein:

you them her you him us you

Kim: Hello, nice to meet you. Can you see Helen? I can't see (1) ______ .

Zoe: No, I can't. But look, there are Tony and Jason. Can you see (2) ______ ?

Tony: Hi girls, nice to meet (3) ______ .

Do you want to come to the park with (4) ______ ?

Kim: No, thank (5) ______ .

Tony: OK. Oh look, there's Gerry.

Jason: Cool, let's talk to (6) ______ . See (7) ______ later, girls!

5 Übersetze die folgenden Sätze.

1. Da ist die Katze. Ich kann sie sehen.

______

2. Da liegt Toms Buch. Bringe ihm bitte sein Buch.

______

3. Kannst du ihr bitte helfen?

______

4. Mary und Karen, könnt ihr mir bitte helfen?

______

6 Übersetze ins Englische und ersetze die unterstrichenen Wörter durch ein Personalpronomen.

1. Thomas wants to read a comic. *He wants to read it.*
2. Mrs Taylor wants to meet Jason. ______
3. The cat sees the mouse in the garden. ______
4. Jacky and Helen like Thomas. ______
5. Mr Jackson reads the newspaper. ______

1 Im folgenden Text fehlen die Formen von to be. Setze die passenden Formen ein.

Look, there (1) ________ a little dog in the garden. The dog's name (2) ________ Sammy.

Sammy and Johnny (3) ________ dogs. They (4) ________ very nice dogs.

This (5) ________ Harry, the cat. Harry and Kitty (6) ________ cool cats.

2 Übersetze ins Englische und ersetze den unterstrichenen Teil des Satzes mit einem passenden Personalpronomen.

1. <u>Karen</u> is a nice girl. ________________________________
2. <u>Gerry and Tim</u> are cool boys. ________________________________
3. <u>The cat</u> is in the garden. ________________________________
4. <u>The cat and the mouse</u> are in the kitchen. ________________________________

3 Setze ein Personalpronomen in der Objektform ein.

1. We want to see *them* (*Tokio Hotel*).
2. We really like ________ (*English*).
3. He gives the book to ________ (*Tony*).
4. Let's talk about ________ (*the weather*).
5. Jason and John want to meet ________ (*Zoe*).
6. Mum, can I phone ________ (*Marco*)?
7. The cat likes ________ (*Collin und Jane*).
8. Can you help ________ (*Kim and me*)?

4 Setze die fehlenden Pronomen in den Text ein:

she his he they him she she it her

Jane is in the house. (1) ________ wants to bake a cake. The cake is a present. It's for Tommy. (2) ________ wants to give (3) ________ to (4) ________ for his birthday. It's (5) ________ birthday on Sunday. Jane is not alone in the kitchen. (6) ________ mother is there, too. (7) ________ is making lunch for the family. (8) ________ are both very busy. John is in the kitchen, too. (9) ________ has a surprise for Jane.

Test 1

5 Beantworte die Fragen mit Kurzantworten.

1. Is he in your class? Yes, ______________.
2. Is she your friend? No, ______________.
3. Are they twelve years old? No, ______________.
4. Is it cold outside? Yes, ______________.
5. Is the cat in your bedroom? No, ______________.
6. Are you hungry? No, ______________.
7. Are you at school at 11 o'clock? Yes, ______________.
8. Are we too loud? No, ______________.

6 Formuliere die Fragen.

1. Frage Bill, ob er aus England kommt.

____

2. Frage Tony und Sally, ob sie in deiner Schule sind.

____

3. Frage Jane, ob sie auch zwölf Jahre alt ist.

____

4. Frage, wo die Tom-Hanson-Schule ist.

____

5. Frage, wer dein Lehrer ist.

____

7 Du triffst einen Austauschschüler aus England. Stelle ihm fünf Fragen z.B. über seine Familie, seine Schule, seine Hobbies oder seine Stadt.

1. Are you ____?
2. ____?
3. ____?
4. ____?
5. ____?

1 Johnny der Frosch und sein Tagesablauf

Johnny gets up at 7 o'clock every morning.

Johnny always brushes his teeth at 7.30.

Johnny and his friend sometimes ride their bikes to school at 8 o'clock.

Johnny often eats lunch at school at 12 o'clock.

Wir benutzen das simple present, wenn etwas ________________ oder ________________ geschieht, z.B. ________________ Tag.

Merke dir Signalwörter: every ________________

He, she, it das 's' muss mit.

Johnny swims in the pond. Aber: Johnny and his friend swim in the pond.

2 Verneinung im simple present. Diese Sätze beschreiben, was man nicht macht oder mag.

a) I don't like computer games.
b) He doesn't do his homework in the morning.
c) Johnny and his friend Swimmy the fish don't play tennis.
d) A lot of pupils in his class don't like Maths.
e) Johnny's teacher doesn't eat lunch at school.

Die Verneinung im simple present bildet man mit ____________ oder doesn't und dem Infinitiv. Man benutzt ____________ nur bei ________, ________, ________.

Simple present

3

Beschreibe deinen Tagesablauf mit den folgenden Verben.

1. to get up — *I always get up at 7o'clock.*
2. to have breakfast ____________________
3. to do homework ____________________
4. to go to bed ____________________

4

Wähle die richtige Form von do und die richtige Verbform aus, unterstreiche sie und schreibe den Satz auf.

1. My mother (don't | doesn't | play | playing) hockey.
   My mother doesn't play hockey.
2. Johnny and Swimmy (doesn't | don't | eating | eat) fish sandwiches.
   ____
3. The pupils in year 5 (doesn't | don't | having | have) a computer in their classroom.
   ____
4. My dad (don't | doesn't | aren't | driving | drives | drive) a motorbike.
   ____

5

Was tun diese Personen und was tun sie nicht?

Peter – eat

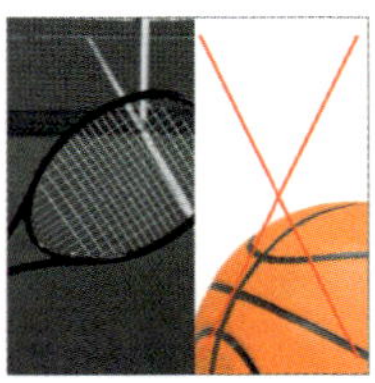

Jane and Sam – play

Tom – to go to school by

My grandma – like

1. *Peter eats pizza but he doesn't eat salad.*
2. ____________________
3. ____________________
4. ____________________

Simple present – **Fragen**

3b

1 Unterstreiche die Fragen blau und die entsprechenden Antworten grün.

Tom: Hello John, do you like the new player in the football team?
John: Hello Tim, yes, I do. He's really good. Hey, come on, let's play football.
Tom: OK. Where do you usually play?
John: We play behind the school on the field. And where do you play football?
Tom: I don't play football very often. Do you have a good ball?
John: Yes, I do, Let's go and get it.

2 Ordne die folgenden Antworten den Fragen zu:
Yes, he does. / Yes, I do. / No, they don't.

1. Do you go to the dance club on Mondays? ______________________
2. Do they play tennis every Saturday? ______________________
3. Does Kevin like basketball? ______________________

3 Hier sind ein paar Fragen, die man einem Austauschschüler stellen könnte.

1. Where do you come from?
2. Who do you invite to your party?
3. What do you like in our town?
4. Why do you like Germany?
5. When do you do your homework?
6. Where do you play hockey?

4 Ordne den Fragen die richtigen Antworten zu.

1. When do you walk to school?
2. Where does Lukas play basketball?
3. Does your dog sit on the sofa?
4. What do they do on Sundays?
5. Do you like the new film ?

a) Yes, we do.
b) No, it doesn't.
c) They always go to the zoo.
d) I walk to school at 7.30.
e) He plays for the Düsseldorf Tigers.

Setze ein: do, does, Infinitiv, do, does, where, when, what
Im simple present werden Fragen mit Vollverben so gebildet:

__________ oder __________ + Subjekt + __________ . Fragewörter wie z.B. __________ , __________ , __________ werden vor das __________ oder __________ gestellt.

Simple present – Fragen

5 Setze die fehlenden Wörter ein.

1. ________ does school start in your town?
2. Where ________ your grandparents live?
3. ________ you want to play with us?
4. ________ ________ you watch on TV?
5. ________ ________ you play computer games?
6. ________ your friend have a computer in his room?
7. ________ you have a cafeteria at your school?
8. ________ ________ you do your homework?

do
does do
do when do
when do when
do what

6 Diese Fragen sind durcheinander geraten. Schreibe sie richtig auf.

1. every day | she | does | drink | coke?

____

2. when | the | arrive | bus | does | at | the | station?

____

3. your | friend | like | does | new | CD | the?

____

4. the | boy | where | new | does | in | class | our | live?

____

7 Beantworte die Fragen.

1. Where do you live? ______________________
2. Does your mother drive a car? ______________________
3. When do you play outside? ______________________
4. Do dogs swim in the sea? ______________________
5. What do you have for breakfast? ______________________
6. Do your parents like pop music? ______________________

1 Beispielsätze (examples) mit dem present progressive.

1. I am reading a book at the moment. 2. She is playing tennis now. 3. Right now they are flying in a plane. 4. Tim isn't sleeping. 5. You aren't watching TV.

2 What are they doing at the moment? Schreibe auf, was die Personen gerade im Moment tun.

1. The dog ______
is eating.

2. The woman ______
______

3. The girl ______
______

4. The boys ______
______

Wir gebrauchen das present progressive, wenn eine oder mehrere Personen, Tiere oder Sachen **jetzt gerade** etwas tun. Das present progressive besteht aus **3 Bausteinen:**

Form von to be (is/am oder are) + ______ + ______.

Suche die Signalwörter des present progressive in den Sätzen von Übung 1 und notiere sie:

______

3 Bei der Bildung der ing- Form sind folgende Schreibweisen zu beachten!

a. She is listening to a cassette. b. She is writing a letter. c. They are run + n + ing.

Setze ein: Buchstabe, ing-Form, Verbs in der Grundform, verdoppelt, ing-Form, Konsonant
Bei der Bildung der ing-Form sind folgende Schreibweisen zu beachten!

a) Die ______ wird an die Grundform des Verbs angehängt.

b) Das ‚e' am Ende des ______ fällt weg und die ______ wird angehängt. c) Endet das Verb in der Grundform auf m, n, t, wird der ______ ______ und die ing-Form angehängt.

Present progressive

4 Schreibe auf, was die Personen auf dem Bild gerade tun.

1. *A boy is cleaning the board.*
2. *A girl*
3.
4.
5.
6.

5 Bilde Sätze mit dem present progressive und den angegebenen Verben.

to eat

to play

to go by

to drive

1. Two girls
2.
3.
4.

Present progressive – **Fragen**

1 Schau dir das Bild an, lies die Fragen dazu und schreibe Kurzantworten.

1. Is the man eating an ice cream? No, he isn't.
2. Are the woman and the girl reading a book? No, they ______
3. Is the woman swimming in the sea? No, ______
4. Is the woman lying in a deckchair? Yes, ______
5. Are the boy and the man playing with a ball? Yes, ______

2 Wie bildet man eine Frage im present progressive?

1. Are they reading an English book? 2. Is the book lying on the table? 3. Am I reading an English book?

Man bildet eine Frage im present progressive mit einer Form von ______ (is / am oder are) + Subjekt + ing- Form.

3 Sortiere die folgenden Wörter und bilde zwei Fragen.

1. you | learning | are | English ______?
2. the dog | is | playing | garden | in | the ______?

Present progressive – **Fragen**

4 Setze die fehlenden Satzteile in die Lücken ein.

visiting is are is going the cat writing are where

1. ________ he playing a game?
2. ________ she ________ to the playground?
3. Are they ________ London?
4. ________ ________ you meeting your friend?
5. Is ________ sleeping in its basket?
6. ________ we ________ a test now?

5 Beantworte die Fragen.

1. Is the bird sitting on a chair? *No, it isn't. It's playing the guitar.*
2. Is the dog running in the garden? ________
3. Is the cat eating a mouse? ________
4. Are the horses sleeping? ________
5. Is the cow standing on the street? ________

6 Bilde Fragen im present progressive.

Is Am Are	I you he/she/it we you they	listen to the music draw a picture buy a new CD sleep on the sofa wash the car talk to your friend

1. *Are they listening to the music?*
2. ________
3. ________
4. ________
5. ________
6. ________

Simple present und *present progressive* im Vergleich

5

1 Unterstreiche die Formen im simple present in blau und die Formen im present progressive in rot.

John:	Jane, what is your brother doing?
Jane:	He is tidying up his room now.
John:	Does he tidy up his room every Saturday?
Jane:	No, he doesn't.
Mrs Peterson:	And what are you doing?
Jane and John:	We are studying for the English test.

Setze ein: often, now, always, right now, sometimes, never, usually, at the moment, every…

Signalwörter für simple present (6): ______________, ______________,

______________, ______________, ______________, ______________,

Signalwörter für present progressive (3): ______________, ______________,

______________________.

2 Unterschied zwischen simple present und present progressive

Thomas is playing a computer game.

It's Monday. Steve and his friend play computer games every Monday.

3 Setze ein Signalwort in die Lücken ein. Es gibt immer mehrere richtige Möglichkeiten .

now   sometimes   at the moment   often   right now

1. My friends ______________ eat ice cream in the afternoon.
2. The pupils ______________ write vocabulary tests.
3. Sam is doing her homework ______________ .
4. Who is listening to CDs ______________ ?

Das present progressive benutzt man, wenn etwas **jetzt im Moment** geschieht.
Das simple present benutzt man, wenn etwas **regelmäßig** oder **immer wieder** geschieht.

Simple present und *present progressive* im Vergleich

4 Setze die Verben in der richtigen Zeit ein. Unterstreiche zunächst das Signalwort im Satz.

1. At the moment the boys ______________________ (*swim*) in the sea.
2. Every Sunday the Smiths ______________________ (*go*) to the zoo.
3. On Mondays Tom ______________________ (*eat*) lunch at his grandma's house.
4. Jill sometimes ______________________ (*play*) computer games with her brother.
5. Jim and John never ______________________ (*talk*) during the English lesson.
6. Our English teacher ______________________ (*clean*) the board at the moment.
7. We often ______________________ (*ride*) our bikes in the park.
8. Grandma ______________________ (*not bake*) a cake at the moment.

5 Simple present oder present progressive? Schau dir den Beispielsatz an und bilde weitere Sätze.

1. Tim | usually | read | a book | on Saturday morning.
   This Saturday morning | he | listen – to a CD.
   Tim usually reads a book on Saturday morning. This Saturday morning he is listening to a CD.
2. Sam and his father | often | go swimming | on Saturday.
   This Saturday | they | play | basketball.
   ____
   ____
3. Mary | sometimes | go | shopping | with | her mother | on Fridays.
   This Friday | they | bake | a cake.
   ____
   ____
4. Mum | usually | listen to the news | in the morning.
   This morning | she | watch | the news | on TV.
   ____
   ____

1 Formuliere Sätze im simple present. Vorsicht bei den Formen der Verben!

1. Monday | go | they | school | to | every

___

2. he | TV | watch | his Dad | with | Tuesday | every

___

3. hockey | school | they | every | play | week | at

___

4. eat | the cat | a mouse | month | every

___

2 Richtig oder falsch? Streiche die falschen Teile durch und korrigiere sie. Welcher Satz ist ohne Fehler?

1. He ~~is playing~~ the guitar every Sunday. ___plays___
2. Peter and Mary jump into the water at the moment. ___
3. Tony is eating pizza on Fridays. ___
4. Right now the cat is sleeping on the chair. ___
5. Every week Mrs Hanson is buying vegetables at the market. ___

3 Setze das Verb im simple present oder im present progressive ein.

1. Timmy ___ (*to see*) his best friend every Wednesday.
2. At the moment Emma and Helen ___ (*to read*) a book.
3. On Sundays the Smiths always ___ (*to go*) to the park.
4. Jason never ___ (*to drink*) milk.
5. The dog ___ (*run*) through the garden now.

4 Übersetze ins Englische.

1. Was machst du gerade? ___
2. Wo spielt ihr montags Fußball? ___

Test 2

5 Beantworte die Fragen mit Kurzantworten.

1. Does she like dogs? Yes, ____________________.
2. Is Tim sleeping? No, ____________________.
3. Are they sitting in the living- room? No, ____________________.
4. Does the TV work? No, ____________________.
5. Is she eating an ice cream? No, ____________________.
6. Do they go by bus? Yes, ____________________.
7. Do we have any homework? Yes, ____________________.
8. Are you cooking? Yes, ____________________.

6 Denke dir eine Antwort zu den Fragen aus. Achte auf die Zeit!

1. When does your best friend go to school on Tuesdays?

____

2. What are the teachers doing at the moment?

____

3. Where do you go every summer?

____

4. When do you usually listen to music?

____

7 Wie lauten die Fragen zu den Antworten?

1. ____

My favourite sport is baseball.

2. ____

Peter always plays basketball on Tuesdays.

3. ____

Jane and Olivia are doing their homework.

Unregelmäßige Verben

1 Was ist ein unregelmäßiges Verb?

Im Englischen ist ein Verb dann unregelmäßig, wenn seine Vergangenheitsform nicht durch ein Anhängen von -ed gebildet wird. Eine Tabelle mit unregelmäßigen Verbformen für das simple past findest du auch hinten in deinem Englischbuch und in diesem Buch auf S. 126.

Setze ein: regelmäßiges – unregelmäßige –ed

To play ist ein ____________ Verb, man hängt im simple past ein ______ an. To do und to buy sind ____________ Verben. Die simple past Formen muss man lernen.

2 Wie lautet die fehlende Form? Kennst du sie? Wenn nicht, schaue in der Tabelle hinten im Buch auf S. 126 nach. Schreibe die entsprechenden Paare auf.

Infinitiv	Simple past	Infinitiv	Simple past
be	*was / were*	*come*	
	did	*make*	
	went		*saw*
have		*run*	

3 Unterstreiche die Verbformen im Text und schreibe sie mit dem passenden Infinitiv auf.

Once upon a time there <u>was</u> a prince and a princess. They lived in a very big castle. They had a horse, a pig, a dog and five cats. On a nice Sunday morning they all went into the woods. There they met the bad witch Alexandra. She lived in a little house out of wood with her six cats and two ravens. Alexandra didn't like the prince and his princess. So she invited them into her little house and said a quiet spell and they became little rats. She put them into a cage and there they lived until they died.

1. *was – be* ____________ 2. ____________ 3. ____________ 4. ____________

5. ____________ 6. ____________ 7. ____________ 8. ____________

9. ____________ 10. ____________ 11. ____________ 12. ____________

13. ____________

Unregelmäßige Verben

4 Unterstreiche das richtige Verb im Satz. Schreibe den ganzen Satz dann auf.

1. Yesterday he *went* | *goed* | *going* | *goes* to school.

____

2. Last week Jason and John *putting* | *put* | *putted* | *puts* a drawing-pin on Tom's chair.

____

3. In my last holidays I *eated* | *eating* | *ate* | *eats* a lot of fish.

____

4. Two years ago I *win* | *winned* | *winning* | *won* a 400 metre race in a championship.

____

5 Schreibe die richtige Form des Verbs im simple past in die Geschichte.

The talking hat

Mary ___had___ (*have*) a little pink hat. It (1) ________ (*be*) a talking hat. One day she (2) ________ (*put*) the hat on the table and (3) ________ (*speak*) to it. She wanted to have a new cool bike. But her parents (4) ______________ (*not have*) enough money. She (5) ________ (*take*) the hat into her hands and wished for a new bike. Woooshhh: there (6) ________ (*be*) a loud noise and she (7) ________ (*see*) smoke in her room. Suddenly there (8) ________ (*be*) a little fairy with a pink dress in her room. Mary (9) ________ (*say*) nothing. Then the little fairy (10) ________ (*sit*) on Mary's hand and smiled. Wooooshhh: there (11) ________ (*be*) a loud noise again and Mary (12) ________ (*see*) a new pink bike. She (13) ________ (*be*) very happy, so she (14) ________ (*give*) the little fairy a kiss. Woooooshhh, and the little fairy (15) ________ (*go*) away. "Thank you so much!" (16) ________ (*say*) Mary. Then she (17) ________ (*take*) her new, pink bike outside and (18) ________ (*show*) it to her friends.

1 Das simple past von to be ist was (für I, he, she, it) und were (für you, we, they). Setze was oder were ein.

1. Yesterday Mum ____________ at Grandma's house.
2. Two weeks ago Tom and Jason ____________ at Grandma's house.
3. Last month Grandma ____________ at our house.
4. In 2004 my parents ____________ in Italy.

2 Bildung des simple past mit regelmäßigen und unregelmäßigen Verben. Übersetze die Sätze.

1. I played with my best friend yesterday.

____

2. Last Saturday I went to the cinema.

____

Das simple past benutzt man, wenn man erzählt, was in der ____________ passierte.
Es gibt folgende Signalwörter: ____

____

Regelmäßige Verben enden im simple past auf – ed. Unregelmäßige Verben haben keine Regel für ihre Bildung, man muss sie einfach lernen. (mehr dazu in Kapitel 6 und auf S. 126)

3 Verneinung

Jim and John didn't see the funny plane. Karen didn't believe Tom. We didn't have orange juice.

Setze ein: verneinten - simple past - didn't (did not) - weren't - wasn't

Im ____________ werden Vollverben mit ____________ + Infinitiv verneint.
Diese Regel gilt für alle Personen. Die ____________ simple past Formen von to be heißen ____________ (Singular) und ____________ (Plural).

Simple past

4 Tom erzählt, was er letzte Woche erlebt hat. Unterstreiche die Verben, die im simple past stehen.

Listen. This crazy story happened last week: I was on my way to school. Suddenly I saw a big light in the sky. It came nearer and nearer. I saw that it was a small vehicle. It looked like a very funny little plane. It landed in the park. Two funny people came out. They said: "Hello, we are Monti and Konti, who are you? We are on our way to Mars and we need some orange juice for our plane. It only works with orange juice!" It was no problem for me because I had a bottle of juice with me. So I gave it to them. They filled it into their plane and flew into the sky again. What a crazy day it was.

5 Unterstreiche das Signalwort und setze dann die Verben richtig ein.

1. Two years ago I ______________________ (*be*) in Greece with my family.
2. Six friends ______________________ (*come*) to my birthday party last weekend.
3. Mr Meyer ______________________ (*give*) us a lot of homework yesterday.
4. Last Monday we ______________________ (*go*) to the bowling centre with our friends.
5. Max and Melanie ______________________ (*watch*) a great film last night.
6. Yesterday I ______________________ (*clean*) all my shoes.

6 Setze Verben ins simple past. Aufgepasst! Manche Verben stehen in der Verneinung!

1. We ______________________ (*not go*) to school last Tuesday.
2. Last week Jack ______________________ (*ride*) his bike to school.
3. I ______________________ (*not get*) a new computer yesterday.
4. The cat ______________________ (*sleep*) in its basket last night.
5. My English teacher ______________________ (*not be*) happy about my last test.
6. Sarah and Jill ______________________ (*not like*) the music at our school party.

Simple past – **Fragen**

1 Die Freunde von Tom stellen ein paar Fragen. Ordne sie den richtigen Antworten von Tom zu.

1. Jessica: Did they look frightened?
2. James: Who saw them, too?
3. Gary: How big was their plane?
4. Helen: When did you see them?
5. Zoe: Where did you meet them?
6. Jim: Were you frightened?

a. My dog saw them, too.
b. No, they looked funny.
c. I saw them on my way to school.
d. It was very, very, very small.
e. No, I was really, really cool.
f. I met them in the park.

2 Fragen mit to do

Fragen im simple past bildet man mit did + Subjekt + Infinitv des Verbs.

Did they look friendly?

Setze die folgenden Wörter zu einer Frage zusammen: you | did | see | them | again?

3 Fragen mit Fragewörtern. Hier sind die Wörter durcheinander geraten. Bring sie in die richtige Reihenfolge.

When	bag	did	do
Who	did	the bag	leave
What	bought	they	go
Which	did	he	for you
Where	did	she	you carry

Nach den Fragewörtern when / why / what / where / who (= wen oder wem?) im simple past steht did.
Nach dem Fragewort who (= wer) steht zuerst das Verb im simple past.
Nach dem Fragewort which steht zunächst das Objekt.

Simple past – **Fragen**

4 Unterstreiche das Signalwort und setze die Wörter ein.

1. ______ they have a lot of homework yesterday?
2. ______ did they meet the boys last months?
3. ______ met her favourite popstar last Sunday?
4. ______ she ______ the cool book last week?
5. ______ ______ my pencil case?

where took did who who buy did

5 Sortiere die Antworten und ordne sie dann jeweils der richtigen Frage zu.

a) 7 o'clock | at | went | they
b) A | an | wrote | Jason
c) she | yes | did
d) didn't | no | they
e) the | met | she | him | library | in
f) CD of | the | she | Tokio Hotel | bought | new

1. Did she like the movie? ______
2. Where did she meet him? ______
3. Which CD did she buy? ______
4. Who wrote an A in his English test? ______
5. Did they talk to Mrs Hanson? ______
6. When did they go to the cinema? ______

6 Stelle Mark fünf Fragen über seinen letzten Urlaub.

1. Frage ihn, ob er im Meer geschwommen ist. ______
2. Frage ihn, ob sie in einem Hotel geschlafen haben. ______
3. Frage ihn, ob er nette Mädchen getroffen hat. ______
4. Frage ihn, ob er ein Schloss gesehen hat. ______
5. Frage ihn, ob er ein Souvenir gekauft hat. ______

1 Setze die Formen der Verben im simple past ein.

1. He ________________ (*go*) to the cinema yesterday.
2. They ________________ (*be*) in France last summer.
3. In 1999 I ________________ (*visit*) my grandma in the USA.
4. The dog ________________ (*run*) through the park.
5. John and Mary ________________ (*not do*) their homework.
6. Helen ________________ (*buy*) a new CD of her favourite pop group yesterday.
7. Jane ________________ (*not like*) the film on TV last night.
8. Thomas ________________ (*not eat*) lunch at home last Monday.
   He ________________ (*eat*) at his grandma's house.
   His grandma ________________ (*cook*) for him.

2 Bringe die Fragen in die richtige Reihenfolge und schreibe sie auf.

1. he | did | play | the | this | piano | afternoon?

____

2. leave | they | did | when | house | the?

____

3. book | did | which | she | want | birthday | her | for?

____

4. did | where | stay | you | class trip | on | the?

____

3 Beantworte die Fragen mit Kurzantworten.

1. Did you like the film? Yes, ____________. 2. Did Max call you? No, ________________. 3. Did they write a class test? No, ________________. 4. Did you tidy up your room? Yes, ____________. 5. Did Mrs Smith shout at you? Yes, ________________. 6. Did you go to the party? No, ________________.

Test 3

4 Erfinde Antworten zu den Fragen.

1. When did you meet him? ______________________________
2. Why did she like him? ______________________________
3. Which class test did you write? ______________________________
4. Who was the man in your kitchen? ______________________________
5. Where did you put your lunchbox? ______________________________

5 Wie lautet die Frage zu den einzelnen Antworten?

1. ______________________________

Yes, I really saw Brad Pitt in the hotel.

2. ______________________________

It was my new English teacher.

3. ______________________________

We left at 7 o'clock in the morning.

4. ______________________________

We slept at a youth hostel last weekend.

6 Finde 12 unregelmäßige simple past-Formen im Wortgitter (waagerecht).

y	o	u	s	a	w	r	o	m	h	a	d	t	z	u	i	b	e	w	a	s	u	i	e	t
r	e	b	o	u	g	h	t	a	t	h	u	r	t	n't	d	r	e	s	h	o	u	t	e	z
j	k	ö	d	r	a	n	k	i	w	e	n	t	h	u	a	t	b	o	t	t	l	e	u	f
o	f	m	i	l	d	i	d	b	n	h	e	p	i	z	s	a	i	d	d	n	s	a	t	a
d	o	t	o	o	k	h	i	s	h	u	l	h	o	m	e	w	o	r	k	ö	c	a	m	e

Schreibe nun die Grundformen zu den 12 unregelmäßigen Verben aus dem Rätsel auf.

____

____

____

Wortstellung in Aussagesätzen

8

1 Der Aufbau eines Aussagesatzes

1. Kevin and Tim can speak German.
2. I am reading a book.
3. The band is playing music.

Subjekt Verb Objekt

2

Achte bei der Übersetzung auf die Unterschiede im Satzbau in den beiden Sprachen. Im Englischen werden die Verben in der Regel **nicht** voneinander getrennt. Es gilt S-V-O!

1. Kevin can't write his name. → Kevin kann seinen Namen nicht schreiben.
2. Mary and Jane must do their homework. → Mary und Jane müssen ihre Hausaufgaben machen.

3 Stellung der Adjektive in einem Satz

1. Kevin is a big football star.
2. I am reading an interesting book.

Weitere Möglichkeiten nach *to be*:

3. Kevin is nice.
4. I was nervous.

TIPP

Adjektive geben zusätzliche Informationen zu Personen / Dingen oder Tieren. Sie stehen entweder **vor dem Nomen** oder **nach** dem Verb ***to be***.

4 Adverbien der Häufigkeit (adverbs of frequency)

1. She often rides her bike to school.
2. They usually play tennis on Mondays.
3. I sometimes travel to France with my family.
4. She never goes to school by bus.
5. We always have breakfast together.

Im simple present Satz stehen Adverbien der Häufigkeit zwischen dem ______________________ und dem ______________________ !

5 Ort vor Zeit

I'm meeting Peter in front of **the cinema** (Ort) **at 6 o'clock** (Zeit).
Ich treffe Peter um 6 Uhr vor dem Kino.

TIPP

Im Englischen gilt Ort vor Zeit!

Wortstellung in Aussagesätzen

6 Bilde Aussagesätze. Bringe die folgenden Satzteile in die richtige Reihenfolge.

1. are | the bus | in | the pupils | sitting

2. have got | Sarah and I | pink | bikes

3. sometimes | goes | Mr Brown | on Saturdays | swimming

4. play | they | often | games | in the evening

5. pool | at | the | meet | every Monday | we | girls | nice | the

7 Adjektiv oder Adverb? Setze ein passendes Wort in die Lücken.
Es gibt mehrere Möglichkeiten.

never always often clever nice quick

1. He ______ takes the bus.
2. They ______ eat frogs.
3. They are ______ girls.
4. Do you ______ go by bike?
5. She is a ______ runner.
6. Look at the ______ cat.

8 Eine geheime Botschaft ist durcheinander geraten. Wie heißt sie?

cafeteria you I meet 8 o'clock the at in

Sie lautet:

Fragewörter

9

1 Unterstreiche im Text die Fragewörter und übersetze sie.

1. Mrs Hobbs: What are your favourite pets? Was
2. Tony: Where is my book? ______
3. Jule: When is the meeting at the pool? ______
4. Michael: How many pens are in your pencil case? ______
5. Sarah: Why is there so much homework, Mrs Jackson? ______
6. Joe: Who is the new girl in our class? ______
7. Becki: Which is your favourite colour? ______

Die meisten englischen Fragewörter beginnen mit Wh (Wh- Wörter), außer how.

TIPP

2 Wie werden Fragen mit Fragewörtern und to be gebildet?

1. What is his favourite meal?
2. Where is he from?
3. When is the lesson over?
4. Why are you in Germany?
5. Who is the man at the desk?
6. Which is your bike?
7. How are you?

TIPP

Fragen in anderen Zeiten findest du in den entsprechenden Kapiteln zu den Zeiten.

3 Ergänze die fehlende Übersetzung.

Englisch	Deutsch
1a. Where is your school?	1b. ______
2a. ______	2b. Wo sind meine Freunde?
3a. Who is the man?	3b. ______
4a. ______	4b. Wer ist der neue Junge?

Verwechsle nicht who und where, denn who heißt im Deutschen ______ und where bedeutet ______ .

Fragewörter

4 Setze die Fragewörter in die Lücken ein. Manchmal gibt es mehrere Möglichkeiten.

why when who where what which

1. ____________ is his birthday?
2. ____________ is your best friend?
3. ____________ are you from?
4. ____________ is the new CD?
5. ____________ is your cat?
6. ____________ are my shoes?
7. ____________ is the girl at the corner?
8. ____________ aren't you at school?
9. ____________ isn't the game interesting?
10. ____________ is he there?
11. ____________ time is it?
12. ____________ are they at home?
13. ____________ is the girl over there?
14. ____________ is in my room?

5 Stelle Lisa ein paar Fragen.

1. Frage, wo ihr Buch ist. ____________
2. Frage, wie es ihr geht. ____________
3. Frage, wann ihr Geburtstag ist. ____________
4. Frage, wo ihr Bruder ist. ____________
5. Frage, was ihr Lieblingslied ist. ____________

6 Finde richtige Fragen mit Fragewörtern in den Wortschlangen. Es gibt mehrere Möglichkeiten.

1. whatwhenisdothetheymeetingatontheabusshopstop

____

2. wherewhoareissheatfrom

____

3. howwhoareamthegirlssheoutainthecorner

____

4. whatwhyisarethedogsondointhegarden

____

Fragen und ihre Antworten

10

1 Hier siehst du verschiedene Fragen in unterschiedlichen Zeiten. Notiere die Zeit, in der sie stehen.

1. Is the girl playing with her dog at the moment? ______
2. Do you like the new Fantasy book? ______
3. What did you do last weekend? ______
4. Why don't you talk to the new teacher? ______
5. Why are they shouting at me? ______

2 Wie lauten die Antworten? Ordne den Fragen die richtigen Antworten zu.

1. Have Peter and Jim got a new computer?
2. Do you like the new Fantasy book?
3. What did you do last weekend?
4. Why do you like the new teacher?
5. Did they write a test last lesson?
6. Is Tina playing with her dog at the moment?
7. Who has got a new bike?
8. Is there any milk in the fridge?

a) We went to Cologne by train.
b) Yes, they have.
c) Yes, I do.
d) I like him because he's so cool.
e) Yes, she's playing with her dog.
f) Yes, there is.
g) Yes, they did.
h) Mary has got a new bike.

3 Beantworte die Fragen. Achte auf die verschiedenen Zeiten.

1. Are your friends having a party at the moment? ______
2. Does your mum go to the pool every Monday? ______
3. Did your teacher jump into the water yesterday? ______
4. Do you like your town? ______
5. Why aren't you sitting next to your best friend? ______
6. When did you learn for the test? ______

Setze die fehlenden Wörter ein: Signalwörter, Zeit, Antwort
Wenn du auf eine Frage antwortest, überlege zuerst, in welcher ______ die Frage steht und schreibe dann die ______ auf. Manchmal helfen dir ______.

Fragen und ihre Antworten

4 Beantworte die Fragen mit Kurzantworten.

1. Did your friends like the hot chocolate? Yes, ____________________.
2. Do you go to school by bus? No, ____________________.
3. Does the dog sleep on the couch at night? Yes, ____________________.
4. Did your sister write a letter to her new boyfriend? No, ____________________.

5 Kate stellt dir ein paar Fragen. Beantworte sie.

1. What did you do last weekend? ____________________
2. Have your parents got a house with a garden? ____________________
3. Which is your favourite subject at school? ____________________
4. Do you like swimming in the sea? ____________________
5. Where do you live? ____________________
6. Are you sitting at a table at the moment? ____________________

6 Hier gibt es technische Probleme bei einem Telefongespräch: Frage nach den fehlenden Informationen!

1. I went to uuppss with my family last summer. *Where did you go last summer?*
2. My hobbies are uuppss and playing uuppss. ____________________?
3. I always go to school at uuppss every Tuesday. ____________________?
4. uuppss has got a flat with a balcony. ____________________
5. I want to go out because uuppss. ____________________?
6. Peter and Karl are going to the uuppss. ____________________?

Präpositionen

11

1 Unterstreiche im folgenden Text die Präpositionen und schreibe sie auf.
Beispiel: The dog is <u>on</u> the table. <u>On</u> ist eine Präposition.

This is my cat. Her name is Kitty. The cat is on the chair. Sometimes Kitty is under the table and in her basket. Her friend is our neighbour's cat Conrad. Conrad is next to the door now. He often is behind the door, too. Sometimes he is under the couch and I am in front of the door.

Die Präpositionen im Text sind: ___on___, ________, ________, ________, ________, ________ und ________.

2 Welche Übersetzung gehört zu welchem Satz. Verbinde!

1. Peter is under the table.
2. Mary is next to the door.
3. The dog is in the basket.
4. The children are in front of the house.
5. The cat is behind the tree.
6. The books are on the table.

in | vor | unter | neben | auf | hinter

3 Schreibe den richtigen Satz zu jedem Bild und benutze die passende Präposition.

1

2

3

4

5

6

1. The book is ___in___ the bag.
2. The book ________________.
3. ________________.
4. ________________.
5. ________________.
6. ________________.

Präpositionen

4 Wo sind die Sachen im Zimmer? Schreibe fünf Sätze zu dem Bild. Benutze Präpositionen.

1. *There is* ______
2. ______
3. ______
4. ______
5. ______

5 Formuliere lustige Sätze mit den folgenden Wörtern.

		in	the pond	1. ______
my teacher	is	**under**	the desk	2. ______
my best friend	are	**behind**	the cupboard	3. ______
my parents		**next to**	my bed	4. ______
my mother		**on**	my school bag	5. ______

6 Beantworte die Fragen.

1

2

3

4

1. Is the frog in the pond? *No it isn't. It's next to the pond.*
2. Is the dog under the bed? ______
3. Are the mice on the chair? ______
4. Is the cat in front of the cupboard? ______

1 Unterstreiche in den Sätzen das Subjekt rot, das Verb grün und das Objekt blau.

1. He reads a book.
2. Our German teacher doesn't speak English.
3. Peter and John are making sandwiches.
4. I didn't understand the text.
5. The cat always drinks milk.
6. Karen doesn't like the new German teacher.

2 Setze ein passendes Fragewort ein. Manchmal gibt es mehrere Möglichkeiten.

1. ______________ do you go to school?
2. ______________ glass is your glass?
3. ______________ are you from?
4. ______________ are you doing?
5. ______________ are you today?
6. ______________ are you crying?
7. ______________ is the girl from London?
8. ______________ are you going?
9. ______________ are the cookies?
10. ______________ time is it?

3 Denke dir Antworten auf die Fragen aus und achte auf die richtige Zeit.

1. Did you see Anna yesterday? ______________________________
2. Are they watching a good movie? ______________________________
3. When do you want to visit me? ______________________________
4. Does your mum have a brother? ______________________________
5. Where is she going to? ______________________________
6. Can we sit here, please? ______________________________

4 Martin war zwei Wochen in den USA. Stelle ihm vier Fragen über seine Reise. Benutze die Fragewörter what, where, when, which, how, why oder who und achte auf die Zeit.

1. ______________________________
2. ______________________________
3. ______________________________
4. ______________________________

Test 4

5 Übersetze ins Englische.

1. auf dem Pult ______________
2. in der Küche ______________
3. unter dem Stuhl ______________
4. neben dem Regal ______________
5. hinter der Tür ______________
6. im Schlafzimmer ______________
7. vor dem Haus ______________
8. vor dem Kino ______________

6 Du machst eine Sportreportage live im Radio. Schreibe die Sätze in der richtigen Zeit auf.

1. John | run | 50 metres 2. Helen and Tom | jump 3. Jane | throw | balls
4. the | the | coach | shout | athletes | at

1. ______________
2. ______________
3. ______________
4. ______________

7 Frage nach den unterstrichenen Satzteilen. Achte auf die unterschiedlichen Zeiten.

1. ______________

We read <u>a good book</u> at school last month.

2. ______________

Susan and Helen go with the dog for a walk <u>every Monday</u>.

3. ______________

The dogs <u>are sleeping</u> in their dog house.

4. ______________

<u>I'm fine, thank you?</u>

5. ______________

We can watch the new Mr Bean film <u>in Stuttgart.</u>

1 Unterstreiche die Formen von can und die Verben.

2 Welche Satzstellung ist richtig? Kreuze den richtigen Satz an.

- a. I can in the house play with my friends.
- b. I can play in the house with my friends.
- c. I can with my friends play in the house.

Can ist ein Hilfsverb und kann nie alleine stehen, es braucht immer noch ein Vollverb. Nach can steht immer der ______________________ .

3 Verneinung mit can

You can't go into the woods alone.
He can't go to Snow White's house.

TIPP Die Langform von can't heißt cannot. Sie wird aber nur selten benutzt.

Auch nach can't / cannot steht immer der ______________________ .

4 Schreibe Sätze mit can / can't.

1. not play | guitar | he: *He can't play the guitar.*
2. write | they | in English: ______________________
3. swim | in the sea | we: ______________________
4. not speak | you | in the Maths lesson: ______________________

TIPP Für alle Personen ist die Form: can / can't + Infinitiv gleich.

Can / can't

5

Setze die fehlenden Formen mit can oder can't ein.

1. I ______ ______ the guitar. (*not play*)
2. Peter and Timmy ______ ______ English songs. (*sing*)
3. Tom ______ ______ his mother in the kitchen. (*help*)
4. We ______ ______ in our classroom. (*not run*)

6

Bilde zwei Sätze mit can und zwei Sätze mit can't. Benutze dabei aus jeder Box ein Element.

my cousin, Mum and Dad, a dog, Tracy	play, help, read, speak

1. ______
2. ______
3. ______
4. ______

7

Schreibe die Sätze auf und benutze can und can't in jedem Satz.

1. Jason	**2. Mary**	**3. Tony and Helen**	**4. The pupils**
speak English	go by bike	play badminton	~~write on a paper~~
~~speak Greek~~	~~drive a car~~	~~play tennis~~	write in exercise books

1. *Jason can speak English, but he can't speak Greek.*
2. ______
3. ______
4. ______

Can you ... ? – Fragen mit *can*

1 Welche Antworten passen zu den Fragen? Verbinde.

Can you help me with my bike, Dad?

Can Kim and Jill bake a cake for Grandma?

Can I play at the computer, Mum?

Can Jason play the piano?

No, you can't.

Yes, he can.

Yes, I can.

No, they can't.

2 Fragen mit can. Schau dir die Beispielsätze genau an und vervollständige dann die Erklärung.

Aussagesatz:	Tina can give you the book.	Marc can buy the camera.
Frage:	Can Tina give you the book?	Can Marc buy the camera?
Frage mit Fragewort:	When can Tina give you the book?	When can Marc buy the camera?

Setze ein: vor, zwischen, nach

Im Aussagesatz steht can __________ dem Subjekt des Satzes.

Bei Fragen, wird can __________ das Subjekt des Satzes gestellt.

Bei Fragen mit Fragewörtern, steht can __________ dem Fragewort und dem Subjekt des Satzes.

3 Welche Frage passt zu welcher Antwort? Schreibe die richtige Frage in die Zeile.

Can you open the window, please?
Can Sandra come to the cinema with us?
Can Mr Grease be nice, too?
Can the cat sleep in your bed?

1. ______________________________ – No, it can't.
2. ______________________________ – Yes, he can.
3. ______________________________ – Yes, I can.
4. ______________________________ – No, she can't.

Can you … ? – **Fragen mit** *can*

4 Finde in jeder Wortschlange eine Frage mit can und schreibe sie auf.

1. docanyourshedancesdancewithtomeI?

2. canhaveyoutheybeisnicebesttoaboutyouryousisterjenny?

3. gocantheythemplayplayingintheasgarden?

4. doescanthemhesitsittingnexttoonmeourin?

5 Denke dir passende Antworten aus und schreibe sie auf.

1. Can you jump three metres?
2. Can old people run 400 metres in one minute?
3. Can your mum lift 100 kg?
4. Can children swim 1 km in 30 minutes?

6 Stelle einer berühmten Person zwei Fragen mit can.

1. Can you run a marathon?
2. Can you
3.

Must / mustn't – needn't

13

1 In jeder Zeile steckt ein Satz mit must / mustn't oder needn't.
Finde die Sätze und schreibe sie auf.

y	o	u	g	o	t	r	o	m	u	s	t	n	z	u	i	b	e	w	e	q	u	i	e	t
r	e	t	t	h	e	y	c	a	t	m	u	s	t	n	't	r	e	s	h	o	u	t	e	z
j	w	e	w	i	z	m	u	s	t	u	s	r	e	a	d	e	a	d	b	o	o	k	u	f
h	e	m	n	e	e	d	n	't	n	h	d	o	i	a	u	t	e	s	t	n	p	o	p	a
s	h	e	j	m	u	s	t	n	't	u	k	p	l	a	y	o	o	u	t	s	i	d	e	l

1. ____________________
2. ____________________
3. ____________________
4. ____________________
5. ____________________

Setze die folgenden Wörter ein: Infinitiv, nicht dürfen, müssen, nicht müssen, nicht brauchen

Die Übersetzung von must ist ______________, mustn't heißt ______________,

und needn't bedeutet ______________ oder ______________.

Nach must / mustn't oder needn't folgt immer ein ______________.

2 Lies die Anweisungen für eine Klassenfahrt. Übersetze die unterstrichenen Wörter.

1. You **must be** in bed at 9 o'clock. Ihr ______________ um 9 Uhr im Bett ______________.
2. You **mustn't bring** a mobile phone. Ihr ______________ kein Handy ______________.
3. You **needn't get up** at 6 o'clock but you **must get up** at 7.30. Ihr ______________ um 6 Uhr ______________, aber ihr ______________ um 7.30 Uhr ______________.
4. Your parents **must come** to the school meeting on Friday afternoon. Eure Eltern ______________ zum Treffen in der Schule am Freitag Nachmittag ______________.

Must / mustn't – needn't

3 Hier sind weitere Anweisungen für die Klassenfahrt. Setze must / mustn't oder needn't ein.

1. The pupils ______________ eat pizza in their rooms.
2. The teachers ______________ knock at the door before they come in.
3. The bus driver ______________ be very nice to the pupils.
4. You ______________ bring towels. There are towels in the bathroom.

4 Formuliere zu den Bildern Sätze mit must oder mustn't .

1

2

3

4

5

1. *You must turn right here.*
2. ______________
3. ______________
4. ______________
5. ______________

5 Schreibe Sätze mit needn't oder must oder mustn't.

1. It's dark and wet outside: Jane | new shoes | wear

Jane mustn't wear her new shoes.

2. It's cold outside: wear | summer jacket | they

____

3. It's hot outside: pupils | homework | do | their

____

4. It's raining outside: Peter and Tim | an | take | umbrella

____

1 Der unbestimmte Artikel a / an

	1. <u>a</u> pencil case	2. <u>a</u> book
ABER:	3. <u>an</u> apple	4. <u>an</u> exercise book

Es heißt a uniform und a unit aber an uncle.

Setze ein: Konsonanten / Vokal / ein, eine

Der unbestimmte Artikel a / an heißt im Deutschen: ____________________.

Man benutzt a, wenn das folgende Wort mit einem **gesprochenen** ____________________ beginnt. Man benutzt an, wenn das folgende Wort mit einem **gesprochenen** ____________________ beginnt.

2 Der bestimmte Artikel the
Übersetze die unterstrichenen Satzteile und ergänze dann die Regel.

1. This is <u>the best pizza</u>. ____________________
2. This is <u>the girl from England</u>. ____________________
3. This is <u>the old man from next door</u>. ____________________

In der englischen Sprache gibt es nur **einen** bestimmten Artikel, und zwar für Singular und für Plural: the. In der deutschen Sprache gibt es __________ Artikel: __________, __________ und __________.

3 Aussprache

Beispiel 1: This is <u>the</u> [ðə] sandwich for Sally.
Beispiel 2: This is <u>the</u> [ði:] apple for Sam.

Vorsicht bei der Aussprache!
Beginnt das Wort nach the mit einem gesprochenen Vokal, wird the mit langem i [ði:] ausgesprochen.

a / an – the

4 Sagt man bei diesen Wörtern [ðə] oder [ðiː]? Ordne die Wörter der richtigen Aussprache zu:

orange chair board apple afternoon unit car bike end exercise guitar idea

[ðə]		[ðiː]	

5 Kreuze an, ob man [ðə] oder [ðiː] sagt.

	[ðə]	[ðiː]
1. I have got the old books from Jason.	●	●
2. She has got the new Disney film.	●	●
3. Has she got the oranges for the drink?	●	●
4. This is the unit from our English book.	●	●
5. This is the new unit from our French book.	●	●

TIPP: Denk daran: die Aussprache des the, und ob man a oder an nimmt, hängt vom Anfangslaut des folgenden Wortes ab.

6 Setze a oder an ein.

1. Peter and Karl have got ______ computer in their room.
2. The pupils in year 5a have got ______ extra sports day at school.
3. They have got ______ rabbit in ______ cage in the garden.
4. It has ______ apple in its mouth.
5. Helen has got ______ TV in her room.
6. We have got ______ English girl in our class and she has got ______ nice brother.

7 Schreibe zehn Dinge auf, die in deiner Schultasche sind und benutze dabei a oder an.

a pencil

____

____

1 Sätze und Fragen mit have got / has got

Sarah: I have got a new iPod.

Jason: Has Mary got a new CD-player?

Jim and Tim: We've got new mobiles!

Man benutzt have got oder has got, wenn man sagen will, dass man etwas besitzt.

2 Lang- und Kurzformen. Lies dir die Beispielsätze oben noch einmal durch. Ergänze dann in der Tabelle die Kurzformen.

Singular		**Plural**	
Langform	Kurzform	Langform	Kurzform
I have got a computer.	I ________ a computer.	We / You / They	We / You / They
You have got a sweet cat.	You ________ a sweet cat.	have got	________
He / She / It has got a black cap.	He / She / It *'s got* a black cap.	a mobile.	a mobile.

3 Verneinung – Ergänze die fehlenden Formen.

Singular

I *haven't got* a computer.

You ________ a sweet cat.

He ________ a black cap.

She ________ a black cap.

It ________ a black basket.

Plural

We / You / They → ________ a mobile.

Setze die fehlenden Wörter ein: have got, has got, haven't got / hasn't got

Es gibt zwei Formen von have got: ________ und ________. Die Verneinung lautet: ________. In Fragen wird das Hilfsverb have vor das Subjekt gestellt.

have got – has got

4 Setze die fehlenden Wörter ein.

1. *Have* you *got* a red car?
2. ____ he *got* an English book?
3. ____ we ____ new chairs?
4. ____ she ____ a new bag?
5. ____ they ____ a nice teacher?
6. ____ I ____ my keys?

5 Setze have got oder has got in die Lücken ein und beantworte die Fragen für dich.

1. *Have* you *got* a new school bag? *No, I haven't. / Yes, I have.*
2. ____ your friends ____ a dog? ____
3. ____ your mother ____ a car? ____

6 Beschreibe, was die Tiere nicht haben.

1

2

3

4

1. ____
2. ____
3. ____
4. ____

7 Stelle deinen Freunden und deiner Familie ein paar Fragen.

1. Frage, ob Tilo einen Hund hat. ____
2. Frage deine Freundinnen, ob sie einen Freund haben. ____
3. Frage deine Eltern, ob sie Zeit haben. ____
4. Frage, ob Nina die neue CD hat. ____

Would like to **und** *want to*

1 In a restaurant

Waiter: Hello, a table for how many people, please?
Mr Ken: We are four people.
Waiter: Here you are, a table for four. And here's the menu.
Mrs Ken: Thank you.
Waiter: What would you like to drink?
Jason: I want to drink a large coke!
Mrs Ken: Jason, that's not polite. Order again, please.
Jason: I would like to have a large coke, please. Is that OK, Mum?
Mrs Ken: Well done. Yes, it's OK, my darling. ☺

Warum soll Jason nicht I want to, sondern I would like to sagen?

____

Ergänze die Regel.

Man benutzt would like to, wenn man ____________________ sein will. I would like to bedeutet ____________________ und I want to bedeutet ____________________.

2 Unterstreiche die Formen des Verbs im Dialog nach would like to und want to.

Setze ein: Verbs, unverändert, ein –s, Infintiv

Nach would like to und want to steht immer der ____________________ des ____________________. Bei he / she / it braucht want ____________________, would bleibt ____________________.

3 Verbinde jeden deutschen Satz mit dem passenden englischen Satz.

1. Deine Mama fragt deinen Freund, ob er etwas trinken möchte.
2. Die Lehrerin fragt, wer vorlesen möchte.
3. Frank möchte unbedingt die neue CD haben.
4. Die Kinder sitzen am Tisch und sind ziemlich hungrig.

a) Mum, we want to eat something.
b) Who would like to read?
c) Would you like to drink a lemonade, Ken?
d) But Dad, I really want this new CD!

Would like to **und** *want to*

4 Bilde zwei Sätze mit would like to und zwei Sätze mit want to. Benutze die vorgegebenen Verben.

dance catch read play a game

1. Peter and Tom ______
2. Mrs Johnson ______
3. The cat ______
4. Conny ______

5 Would like to oder want to? Setze ein.

1. **Teacher:** I ______ have some of your exercise books.
2. **Sam:** But Muuuuuummmmmm, I ______ have chocolate.
3. **Tom to Tim:** My brother ______ buy a new computer.
4. **In the cafe:** My daughter ______ drink a hot chocolate, please.

6 Drücke die folgenden Sätze höflicher aus.

1. Stewardess in the plane: What do you want to drink?

______

2. Jason wants to have a new bike.

______

3. In a fish and chips shop: I want to eat fish and chips.

______

1 Setze die richtige Form von can oder can't und das Verb ein.

1. Tony and Tim ______________________ (*not write*) a letter in English.
2. They ______________________ (*jump*) into the pool.
3. Johnny ______________________ (*not sing*) the songs of Tokio Hotel.
4. ____________ you ____________ (*give*) me the butter, please?
5. ____________ you ____________ (*be*) quiet, please?

2 Jills Regeln für ihr Zimmer sind durcheinander geraten. Ordne sie wieder!

1. brothers | come in | mustn't *Brothers mustn't come in.*
2. at me | mustn't | shout | you ______________________
3. knock | at the door | you | must ______________________
4. you | bring | needn't | chocolate ______________________
5. nice | parents | be | in | must | room | my ______________________

3 Die Kinder planen einen Ausflug. Setze must / mustn't oder needn't ein.

1. Peter ____________ bring his new knife because we want to make bows and arrows.
2. The children ____________ stay in the woods after 9 o'clock at night.
3. They ____________ get up early, they can sleep until 9 o'clock.
4. Thomas and Karen ____________ bring two camping chairs, so we can all have a picnic.

4 At school – Setze a oder an ein.

At my school there are (1) _____ lot of nice pupils. Today I've got (2) _____ orange and (3) _____ packet of juice in my bag. It's July. There is (4) _____ family day at school every July. Look, Helen has got (5) _____ old school bag from her grandma. Some pupils have got (6) _____ surprise for everybody. It's (7) _____ exciting day.

Test 5

5

Musst du bei diesen Wörtern [ðə] oder [ðiː] sagen? Suche jeweils drei Beispiele aus und schreibe sie in die Tabelle:

pencil case old pencil case apple book exercise book table unit chair English girl girl

[ðə]	[ðiː]
1. ______	4. ______
2. ______	5. ______
3. ______	6. ______

6

Brauchst du bei diesen Wörtern a oder an? Sortiere die Wörter in die Tabelle ein.

boy egg ice cream toast unit orange

a	an

7

Denke dir passende Antworten oder passende Fragen aus.

1. Have you got a cat? ______
2. Has Peter got a new CD? ______
3. ______ No, I haven't got a new bike.
4. ______ Yes, Jane has got a new dog.

8

Finde passende Sätze zu den Situationen und benutze dabei would like to oder want to.

1. Kim will schwimmen gehen.

Kim wants to go swimming.

2. Jason sagt seiner Mutter, dass er mit seinen Freunden Fußball spielen will.

______

3. Mrs Peterson möchte ein Zimmer reservieren und ruft in einem Hotel an.

______

Singular – Plural

1 Verbinde das Wort im Singular mit dem entsprechenden Wort im Plural.

bike, mouse, cherry, sandwich, dog, box, table, fish, ferry, child, foot, sheep, woman, class, country, postcard

postcards, mice, posters, classes, sandwiches, countries, women, cherries, children, sheep, ferries, fish, tables, boxes, dogs, feet, bikes

Lies die Regeln und füge jeweils ein geeignetes Paar von oben als Beispiel hinzu.

1. Man bildet die Pluralform, indem ein -s angehängt wird. Beispiel: ____________________
2. Aus einem -y am Ende wird –ies. Beispiel: ____________________
3. Es wird ein ganz neues Wort gebildet. Beispiel: ____________________
4. Das Wort hat im Singular und im Plural die gleiche Form. Beispiel: ____________________

2 Sortiere die Paare aus Übung 1 in die Tabelle ein. Kennst du weitere Beispiele?

regelmäßig + s	unregelmäßig (neues Wort)	y → ies	Konsonant (s,ch,x) + es	Singular = Plural
____________	____________	____________	____________	____________
____________	____________	____________	____________	____________
____________	____________	____________	____________	____________
____________	____________	____________	____________	____________

Singular – Plural

3 Welches Wort fehlt? Finde ein passendes Wort und setze es im Plural in die Lücke.

fish foot CD child sheep mouse cat country

1. Look, there are two ______________________ in the pond.
2. Two black ______________________ are in the basket in the kitchen.
3. We are three ______________________ in my family.
4. My uncle has got a farm. He has got twenty ______________________ .
5. Aaaaaaahhhhhh, there are four ______________________ on the floor.
6. We are three girls. Together we have got six ______________________ .
7. I like to listen to my new ______________________ .
8. Germany and France are two ______________________ in Europe.

4 Schreibe die Singular- und Pluralformen der gezeigten Bilder auf.

1 
2 
3 
4 
5 
6 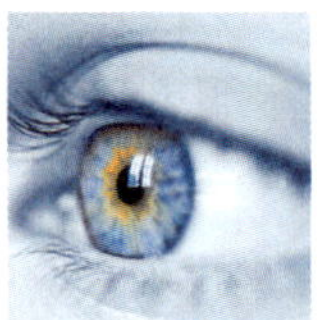
7 
8 

1. ______________________ 2. ______________________
3. ______________________ 4. ______________________
5. ______________________ 6. ______________________
7. ______________________ 8. ______________________

5 Übersetze die folgenden Pluralformen.

1. elf alte Frauen: ______________________
2. acht junge Familien: ______________________
3. drei nette Nachbarn: ______________________

1 Beschreibe das Bild und vervollständige die Sätze.

1. Look, there are four eggs on the table.
2. There is a cup on the table.
3. ________ a knife on the table.
4. ________ one book on the table.
5. ________ a bag on the chair.
6. ________ two plates on the table.
7. ________ a dog on the floor.
8. ________ comics on the floor.
9. ________ a table in the kitchen.
10. ________ chairs in the kitchen.

Setze ein: there is / there are – Dinge – Singular – Plural
Mit ________ kann man auf Personen oder ________ hinweisen.
Im ________ benutzt man there is oder kurz there's: Im ________ benutzt man there are. Im Deutschen sagt man **es gibt** oder **(es) ist** oder **(es) sind**.

2 Was bedeutet there is / there are in diesen Sätzen? Übersetze.

1. There is a new bed in my room. In meinem Zimmer ________ ein neues Bett.
2. There are three chairs in the kitchen. In der Küche ________ drei Stühle.
3. There are three chairs in the kitchen. ________ drei Stühle in der Küche.

Wenn du sagen willst, dass es etwas gibt oder nicht gibt, dann benutzt du dazu im Englischen there is / isn't oder there are / aren't.
There is lots of ice cream. – Es gibt viel Eis.
There aren't any tickets. – Es gibt keine Karten.

There is – there are

3 At the zoo. Setze there is oder there are ein.

1. ______ two lions in the cage.
2. ______ six rats in the box.
3. ______ a kangaroo outside.
4. ______ a big snake behind the glass.
5. ______ four elephants in the zoo.
6. ______ four black spiders on the tree.
7. ______ a funny giraffe at the pond.
8. ______ six monkeys in the monkey house.

4 Du hast einen Bauernhof. Beschreibe, wie viele Tiere auf deinem Bauernhof leben. Schreibe die Zahlen aus.

1. 4 – pig: *There are four pigs on my farm.*
2. 6 – sheep: ______
3. 1 – cat: ______
4. 1 – dog: ______
5. 3 – goose: ______
6. 2 – rabbit: ______
7. 10 – chicken: ______

5 Wo könnten in einem chaotischen Kinderzimmer diese Dinge liegen?

1. *There are four dirty socks on the bed.*
2. ______ an old piece of cheese under the bed.
3. ______ ten comics ______ .
4. ______ dirty plate ______ .

1 Much, many und a lot of in Fragen und Antworten. Verbinde die Fragen mit passenden Antworten.

1. Peter: Are there **many** nice **girls** in your class?

2. Jane: **How much money** have you got?

3. Becki: Mum, have you got an apple for me, please?

4. Katie: **How many boys** are in your class?

a) Mum: Yes, Dear, there are **a lot of apples** in the kitchen.

b) Helen: There are **twelve boys** in my class.

c) Tom: Yes, there are **a lot of** nice **girls** in my class.

d) Carl: Carl: I've got **a lot of** money, I've got £ 2.50!

Setze ein: nicht zählbaren Substantiven / zählbaren Substantiven

Much steht vor ______________________________, und many steht vor ______________________________. Beide werden hauptsächlich in Fragen und verneinten Sätzen benutzt. In bejahten Sätzen wird dagegen meistens a lot of oder lots of benutzt.

2 Setze much oder many ein.

How much is it?
Wie teuer ist es?
Wie viel kostet es?

1. How __________ pocket money do you get? – I get £ 7 per week.
2. How __________ milk have we got in the fridge? – There is only one bottle.
3. How __________ pupils are in your class? – There are 30 pupils in my class.
4. How __________ books are in your school bag? – There are four books in my bag.

3 Setze much, many oder a lot of ein.

1. Jason hasn't got __________ cool clothes.
2. How __________ little dogs are in the basket?
3. I have got __________ cheese on my bread.
4. Peter has got __________ books.

Much – many – a lot of

4 Übersetze die unterstrichenen Wörter.

1. How <u>many friends</u> does Jane have? ______________
2. My grandma hasn't got <u>much money.</u> ______________
3. There are <u>a lot of pigs</u> on the farm. ______________
4. There's <u>a lot of sugar</u> in my tea. ______________

5 Setze much, many oder a lot of ein.

1. Paul and Paula have got ______________ toys in their room.
2. Has James got ______________ animals on his farm?
3. Mrs Peterson has got ______________ tea left.
4. Oh, that shirt is very expensive. That's too ______________ money for me.
5. I want to drink a coke, but there's not ______________ left in the bottle.
6. Do you know how ______________ cats your Aunt Terry has got?

6 Du bist in einem Zeitschriftenladen. Schreibe die englischen Fragen auf und benutze much oder many!

1. Du fragst, wie viel ein Comic kostet.

____

2. Du fragst, wie viele Batman-Comics sie haben.

____

3. Der Verkäufer fragt, wie viele Comics du kaufen möchtest.

____

4. Der Verkäufer fragt, wie viel Geld du hast.

____

This – that / these – those

1 Zwei Mädchen auf Shopping-Tour! Unterstreiche im Text this / that oder these / those und finde die passende Übersetzung rechts.

1. **Stacy:** Look at this nice T-shirt. It's great, isn't it?	a) das blaue T-Shirt da drüben
2. **Mary:** Yeah, but that blue T-shirt over there is nice, too.	b) die Jeans hier
3. **Stacy:** And look, these jeans, aren't they cool?	c) die schwarze Jeans da drüben
4. **Mary:** Yes, but those black jeans over there are great, too.	d) dieses schöne T-Shirt

Setze ein: that – these – this – those

Man benutzt ______________ und ______________ für Dinge, die in der Nähe sind.

Man benutzt ______________ und ______________ für Dinge, die weiter entfernt sind.

TIPP

Here ist ein Signalwort für this / these.
There ist ein Signalwort für that / those.

2 Entscheide, ob man this, that, these, those und here oder over there einsetzen muss.

1. ______________ books here are very interesting.
2. ______________ table here is new.
3. ______________ CD over there is wonderful.
4. This comic ______________ is funny.
5. Those boys ______________ are so sweet.
6. These girls ______________ are very cool.
7. ______________ boy here is new in our class.
8. ______________ woman over there is my teacher.

This und that wird für den Singular benutzt, these und those für den Plural.

This – that / these – those

3 Setze this, that oder these, those ein.

1. I like ______________ shirt here, but I don't like ______________ shirts over there.
2. Toni likes ______________ boy over there very much.

4 Setze ein: this – that – these – those

1. Oh, I love ______________ shoes here.
2. ______________ book over there is very expensive.
3. ______________ girl here is from my class.
4. ______________ boys over there are from another school.
5. ______________ dog here is so funny, but ______________ dogs over there are naughty.

5 Wähle die richtige Form aus.

1. **Mother:** Kevin, would you like that | these comics here or these | those over there?
2. **Kevin:** I would like to have these | this Spiderman comics, please.
3. **Mother:** OK. And do you like this | these cake?
4. **Kevin:** No, I like that | those cake over there.
5. **Mother:** Are those | that girls over there at your school?
6. **Kevin:** No, those | that over there aren't. But this | these girl here is.

S-Genitiv und *of*-Genitiv

21

1 Der s-Genitiv. Schau dir die Sätze an und vervollständige dann die Regel.

1. This is Sarah's CD player.
2. These are the girls' pullovers.
3. This is Steven's bike.
4. This is the cat's biscuit.

Setze ein: Personen und Tieren, Zugehörigkeit

Der s-Genitiv zeigt die ______________________ zu ______________________ ______________ an. Das bedeutet, dass man den s-Genitiv immer dann benutzt, wenn etwas zu einer Person oder zu einem Tier gehört.

2 Der s-Genitiv und die Pluralformen. Ein Beispielsatz in Übung 1 steht im Plural. Welcher ist es? Schreibe ihn auf.

____

3 Schau dir die Sätze an und vervollständige dann die Regel.

The boys' skateboards are new. — Die Skateboards <u>der</u> Jungen sind neu.
The Smiths' car is new. — Das Auto <u>der</u> (auch: von) Smiths ist neu.

Setze ein: Apostroph, s, Pluralformen

Der s-Genitiv gilt auch bei ______________________, die auf __________ enden. In solchen Fällen wird nach dem -s nur noch ein ______________________ angehängt.

4 Der of-Genitiv. Lies die Beispielsätze durch und unterstreiche das Wort, das vom of-Genitiv beschrieben wird.

1. The colour of the table is blue.
2. This is the door of our house.
3. The name of the street is Hill Street.
4. The prices of the T-shirts are high.

Setze ein. Zugehörigkeit, Sachen, Gegenständen

Der of-Genitiv dagegen zeigt die ______________________ zu ______________________ und ______________________ an, im Singular und im Plural.

S-Genitiv und *of*-Genitiv

5 Setze 's oder ' ein.

1. This is Peter___ cat.
2. These are the boys___ skateboards.
3. These are our neighbours___ dogs.
4. This is the cat___ toy.
5. This is the girls___ hamster.
6. These are Jason___ books.
7. These are the dog___ biscuits.
8. This is the teacher___ desk.
9. This is the boys___ room.
10. These are the children___ lunchboxes.

6 Bilde Sätze mit dem of-Genetiv.

1. best computer game | year: *This is the best computer game of the year.*
2. teachers | our school: These are ___
3. garden | our house: ___
4. books | old library: ___

7 Übersetze die folgenden Ausdrücke. Hier siehst du, wie wichtig die Stellung des Apostrophs ist.

1. my brother's friend – *der Freund meines Bruders*
2. my brothers' friend – ___
3. my brothers' friends – ___
4. my brother's friends – ___
5. the dogs' basket – ___
6. the dog's baskets – ___
7. the dogs' baskets – ___
8. the dog's basket – ___

Possessivbegleiter

22

1 In the classroom. Übersetze die unterstrichenen die Wörter.

1. **Tim:** Hi Sarah, is this your new school bag? ______
2. **Sarah:** Yes, it is. And this is my new pencil case. ______
3. **Jane:** Look, our classroom has got new windows. ______
4. **Tommy:** And there is Mrs Peterson. Her new jeans are really cool. ______
5. **Tim:** Kevin is happy. His new iPod is really fantastic, too. ______

Setze ein: etwas, gehört, wem
Die Possessivbegleiter zeigen an, ______ ______ ______.

2 Vorsicht bei den folgenden Formen!

1. This is its new cage. It's very nice. 2. Where is your homework? You're very late.

Its bedeutet ______.

It's besteht aus ______ und ______. Es bedeutet ______.

Your bedeutet ______.

You're besteht aus ______ und ______. Es bedeutet ______.

3 Setze die fehlenden Personalpronomen und Possessivbegleiter in die Tabelle und übersetze sie.

Englisch		Deutsch	
I	my	ich	mein
		du/Sie	
he			
	its		
	your		
they			

Possessivbegleiter

4 Setze die entsprechenden Possessivbegleiter ein:

our your my their my

1. **Janet:** I'm sad. ________ father is without a job. What about ________ father?
2. **Peter and Tim:** We're lucky. ________ father has got a job.
3. **Thomas:** Look at the photo. This is ________ family.
4. **Andrew:** Is this the Petersons' house? Jane: Yes, it's ________ house.

5 Setze ein:

they're their you're your its it's

1. Sven and Helen are new in my class. ________ from London. ________ new books are on Mrs Jason's desk.
2. Jim has got a new dog. ________ favourite place is in his room.
3. Olivia has got a new pullover. ________ wonderful.
4. Tim: Peter, ________ my best friend. ________ jokes are always very funny.

6 Unterstreiche den richtigen Possessivbegleiter im zweiten Satz.

1. Peter and James have got one room: It's our | their | his | her room.
2. Thomas has got a new dog. It's her | its | his | their first dog.
3. The dog has got a new basket. It is his | her | its | our third basket.
4. The Petersons have got a new house. It's their | her | our | his first house.
5. Hey, you, is this your | his | her | our | their new bike?

7 Übersetze die Fragen. Achte auf die unterstrichenen Wörter.

1. Können Sie mir <u>Ihr</u> Haus zeigen? ________________________________
2. Könnt ihr mir <u>eure</u> Bleistifte geben? ________________________________
3. Ist das <u>dein</u> Hund? ________________________________

Aufforderungen und Verbote

1 Sam ärgert seine kleine Schwester Jenny.
Unterstreiche die Imperative (Befehlsformen) im Dialog.

Sam: Jenny, come here.
Jenny: Yes, what's wrong?
Sam: Clean the kitchen before Mum comes home.
Jenny: OK.
Sam: Jenny, get me a hot chocolate.
Jenny: Just a minute.
Sam: Jenny, bake a cake for us.
Jenny: AHHHHHHHH, Sam, I'm not your slave! Shut your big mouth or …
Sam: OK, it was only a joke.

2 Wie bildet man einen Befehlssatz? Lies die Beispielsätze und ergänze die Regel.

Give me the book.
Go home.
Get ten bars of chocolate for me.

Im Englischen steht nach Befehlen **kein** Ausrufezeichen.

Setze ein: Verbs – Imperativ – Infinitiv

Der ________________ wird mit dem ________________ des ________________ gebildet.

3 Befiehl deinem Bruder dein Fahrrad zu putzen und deiner Schwester dein Zimmer aufzuräumen.

1. ______________________________

2. ______________________________

4 Verbote im Klassenzimmer

1. *Don't shout into class.*
2. *Don't eat in the classroom.*
3. *Don't cheat in the class test.*
4. *Don't copy your friend's homework.*
5. *Don't hit other pupils.*

Setze ein: Imperativ – Infintiv

Der verneinte ________________ (Verbot) wird mit don't und dem ________________ gebildet.

Aufforderungen und Verbote

5 Schreibe Befehle auf.

1. go | room | to | your ______________________
2. them | bring | coffee | two cups of ______________________
3. our | clean | cage | budgie's ______________________

6 Setze einen Imperativ ein.

1. (*go*) ___Go___ to the kitchen.
2. (*not eat*) ___Don't eat___ with your hands.
3. (*not get up*) ______________ too late.
4. (*close*) ______________ window.
5. (*do*) ______________ your homework.
6. (*not throw*) ______________ the ball in the house.

7 Schreibe ein passendes Verbot oder einen Befehl auf!

1

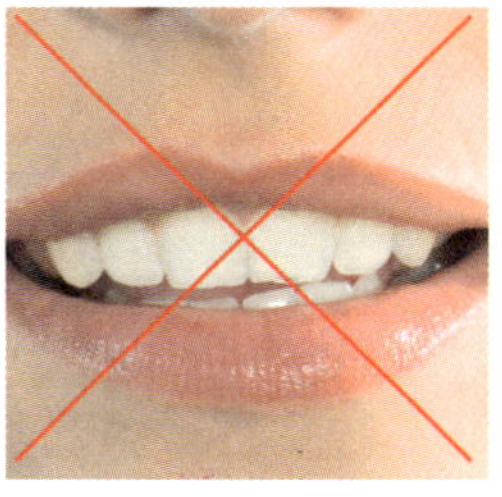

2

3

4

5

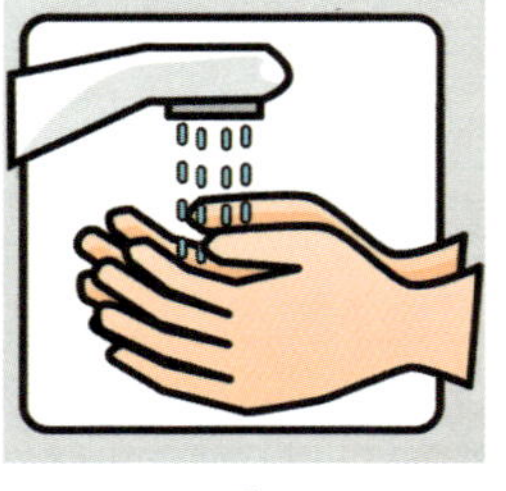

6

1. ______________________
2. ______________________
3. ______________________
4. ______________________
5. ______________________
6. ______________________

1 Finde die Pluralformen in den Wortschlangen und schreibe sie auf.

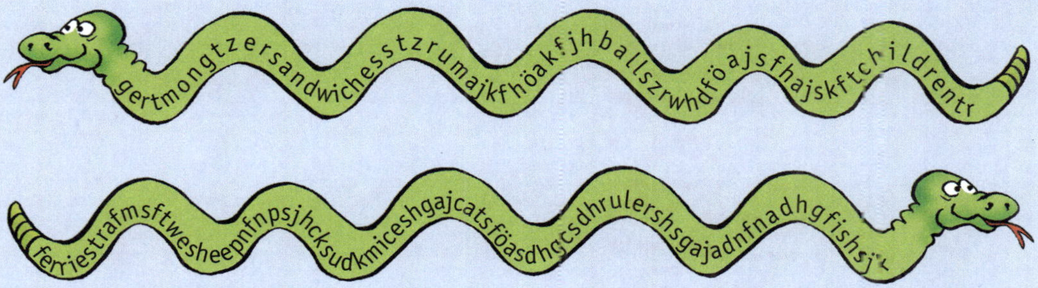

(1) ____________ (2) ____________ (3) ____________

(4) ____________ (5) ____________ (6) ____________

(7) ____________ (8) ____________ (9) ____________

2 Setze there is / there are ein.

Look at our house. (1) ____________ four rooms downstairs and three rooms upstairs. (2) ____________ a room for me, too. (3) ____________ four people in our house and (4) ____________ one dog. Her name is Jacky. (5) ____________ four cats, too. We love animals. Behind the house (6) ____________ a pond in our garden. (7) ____________ ten fish in the pond.

3 Setze in die Lücken much oder many oder a lot of ein.

1. I haven't got ____________ money but I have got ____________ wishes.
2. There isn't ____________ coke in the bottle but there are ____________ bottles in the fridge.
3. There aren't ____________ cool boys but there are ____________ cool girls in my class.
4. There are ____________ children in the park and ____________ dogs, too.
5. I haven't got ____________ time because I have got ____________ things to do.

Test 6

4 Übersetze die folgenden Sätze und benutze this / that oder these / those und here oder over there.

1. Die CDs hier sind meine Lieblings-CDs.

____

2. Die CD da drüben ist auch klasse.

____

3. Die Mädchen und Jungen da drüben sind wirklich nett.

____

5 Bilde Sätze mit dem of- oder dem s-Genitiv.

1. Peter | is | book | this ______________________________
2. the | colour | green | house | is ______________________________
3. is | the neighbours | car | this ______________________________
4. brown | cat | basket | the | is ______________________________

6 Setze die passenden Possessivbegleiter ein.

1. Jason and Tim have got new bikes. ____________ new bikes are green and red.
2. The cat has got a new basket. ____________ basket is big and warm.
3. Helen has got a new dog. It's ____________ second dog.
4. We have got a house with a garden but ____________ neighbour hasn't got a garden.

Verbindungswörter

1

Textgestaltung mit and, or, but, so oder because. Lies die beiden Texte.

Text 1

The little rabbit Carl is in his house. He is eating lunch. Someone is knocking at the door. He opens it. It's his friend, the little hedgehog Sammy. They want to do something. Carl and Sammy don't want to go swimming. It's boring. The two friends don't want to work in the house. They don't want to work in the garden. They want to have a little party with their friends Tilly, the fox, Otto, the mouse.

Text 2

The little rabbit Carl is in his house and is eating lunch. Someone is knocking at the door, so he opens it. It's his friend, the little hedgehog Sammy. They want to do something. Carl and Sammy don't want to go swimming because it's boring. The two friends don't want to work in the house or in the garden. They want to have a little party with their friends Tilly, the fox and Otto, the mouse.

1. Unterstreiche im zweiten Text die Verbindungswörter, die den ersten Text verändert haben.
2. Welcher Text gefällt dir besser? Begründe deine Meinung.

____

2

Was bedeuten die Wörter? Schreibe die deutsche Übersetzung in die Tabelle.

Englisch	Deutsch
and	(1) ____________
but	(2) ____________
so	(3) ____________
because	(4) ____________
or	(5) ____________

TIPP

Mit Verbindungswörtern wie and, but, because und or kann man kurze Sätze miteinander verbinden. Dadurch fließt der Text besser.

3

Welches Verbindungswort passt hier? Setze ein.

1. Yesterday I went into town ____________ I bought a new, cool shirt.
2. My mother isn't at home tonight, ____________ I can stay up late.
3. I like chocolate ice cream, ____________ I don't like strawberry ice cream.
4. Do you want to play football ____________ watch TV?
5. Kim's parents bought a new bike ____________ the old bike was too small.

Verbindungswörter

4 Schreibe Sätze mit but.

1. Ken | play | can | tennis • can't | he | table tennis | play

Ken can play tennis but he can't play table tennis.

2. Jenny and Tom | like | English • not like | they | Geography

3. Tim | comics | read • not read | he | books about | Germany

4. Cats | eat | mice • frogs | not like | them

5 Verbinde die beiden Sätze miteinander und benutze ein Verbindungswort.

1. She plays computer games every afternoon. She doesn't play at night.

2. Peter eats pizza. He also eats hamburgers with a lot of cheese.

6 Beende die Sätze und benutze dabei die Verbindungswörter because, and, so, but oder or.

1. My family likes family games ______
2. I can jump into the water ______
3. It's very nice outside ______

Zahlen bis 100 – Ordnungszahlen

25

1 Die Zahlen von 0 bis 100! Ergänze die fehlenden Zahlen.

1. 0 oh / zero	2. 13 ______	3. 56 ______
4. 1 ______	5. 22 twenty-two	6. 75 ______
7. 3 ______	8. 30 ______	9. 88 ______
10. 12 ______	11. 40 ______	12. 99 ______

TIPP

Einerzahlen werden ab 20 mit einem Bindestrich angehängt: twenty-one, etc. Besondere Schreibweisen bei folgenden Zahlen: 15 - fifteen, 20 - twenty, 40 - forty, 50 - fifty.

2 In einem Schwimmwettkampf haben die Kinder verschiedene Plätze belegt. Setze ein: fourth - fifth - third

Platz 1: Helen, Platz 2: Jason, Platz 3: Karen, Platz 4: Kim, Platz 5: Jenny, Platz 9: Carl

Helen: I'm first. **Jason:** I'm second. **Karen:** I'm (1) ______.

Kim: I'm (2) ______. **Jenny:** I'm (3) ______. **Carl:** I'm ninth.

1., 2., 3. heißen im Englischen: ______, ______,

______

Bei allen anderen Ordnungszahlen hängt man nur ein *-th* an die Grundzahl. Besondere Schreibweisen: **9th - ninth** oder **12th - twelfth und 20th - twentieth**. Diese muss man lernen.

3 Jemand möchte eine Telefonnummer wissen.

TIPP

Wenn z.B. in einer Telefonnummer eine Zahl doppelt vorkommt, sagt man double two und nicht two two.

My telephone number is: (02213)-12345589

"oh-double two-one-three- ______ - ______ -three-four- ______

______ -eight- ______"

Zahlen bis 100 – Ordnungszahlen

4 Was passt zusammen? Verbinde.

13th
31
17
3.
54
70
47
30.
22.

third
seventeen
fifty-four
thirty-one
thirteenth
thirtieth
forty-seven
twenty-second
seventy

5 Schreibe die Zahlen auf, die den Worten entsprechen.

1. thirty-six ____________
2. sixty ____________
3. twelve ____________
4. seventeen ____________
5. fourteen ____________
6. forty-five ____________
7. twenty ____________
8. eighty-seven ____________
9. ninety-three ____________

6 Schreibe die Zahlen als Wort.

1. 19 ____________________
2. 13 ____________________
3. 15 ____________________
4. 25 ____________________
5. 78 ____________________
6. 99 ____________________
7. 67 ____________________
8. 81 ____________________

7 Vier Freunde wollen ein Spiel spielen. Finde heraus, in welcher Reihenfolge sie spielen wollen.

1. Tim: I am after the first person.
2. John: I am after the third person.
3. Helen: I am after the second person.
4. Jane: I am the first.

1. ____________________
2. ____________________
3. ____________________
4. ____________________

Die Uhrzeit

26

1 Wie spät ist es? What time is it? Welches Bild passt zu welchem Satz?
Schreibe die Nummer in das Kästchen hinter den Satz.

1 2 3 4 5

- [ ] a) It's **half past five**. *oder* It's **5.30/five thirty**.
- [ ] b) It's **quarter past** two.
- [ ] c) It's **quarter to** two.
- [ ] d) It's **seven o'clock.**
- [ ] e) It's **twenty past** twelve.

Setze ein: Viertel nach, Viertel vor, minutes, to, past, Stunden, o'clock

Bei Uhrzeiten zwischen voller und halber Stunde benutzt man: ____________ .

Bei Uhrzeiten zwischen halber und voller Stunde benutzt man: ____________ .

Den Begriff ____________ benutzt man nur bei vollen ____________ .

Quarter to heißt ____________ , quarter past heißt ____________ .

Bei Minuten zwischen den Fünferschritten muss man zusätzlich ____________ sagen.

Wenn man im Englischen sagt: It's half five. ist damit 5.30 Uhr gemeint, also halb sechs und **nicht** halb fünf.

2 Welche Uhrzeit gehört zu welchem Satz?

a) 6.30 b) 5.00 c) 4.25 d) 12.53 e) 2.17 f) 11.15 g) 10.45 h) 7:25

- [ ] 1. It's five o'clock.
- [ ] 2. It's quarter past eleven.
- [ ] 3. It's twenty-five past four.
- [ ] 4. It's seventeen minutes past two.
- [ ] 5. It's seven minutes to one.
- [ ] 6. It's twenty-five past seven.
- [ ] 7. It's half past six.
- [ ] 8. It's quarter to eleven.

Die Uhrzeit

3 Schreibe die Uhrzeit auf.

1. It's quarter past six. ______
2. It's twenty-four minutes past three. ______
3. It's half past seven. ______
4. It's twenty-six minutes to eleven. ______
5. It's five to eight. ______
6. It's twelve o'clock. ______
7. It's quarter to nine. ______
8. It's nineteen minutes past eleven. ______

4 Wo steckt der Fehler? Streiche den Fehler durch und schreibe den Satz danach richtig auf.

1. 7.30 It's seven-thirty o'clock. ______
2. 4.30 It's half past five. ______
3. 1.35 It's twenty-five past two. ______
4. 9.15 It's quarter to nine. ______

5 Bringe die Wörter in die richtige Reihenfolge und schreibe den ganzen Satz auf. Gib dahinter in Klammern die Uhrzeit an.

1. five | it's | o'clock: *It's five o'clock.* (*5* : *00*)
2. to | quarter | ten | it's: ______ (___ : ___)
3. twenty-five | it's | past | twelve: ______ (___ : ___)
4. half | past | it's | six: ______ (___ : ___)
5. quarter | past | it's | eight: ______ (___ : ___)

1 Setze passende Verbindungswörter wie so, and, but, because oder or in den Text ein. Manchmal gibt es mehrere richtige Möglichkeiten.

These are my best friends Tony and Chris. They are twelve (1) ______________ thirteen. Today is Saturday (2) ______________ we want to have a nice day in town. The sun is shining, (3) ______________ we don't want to go swimming. We want to drive into town (4) ______________ meet our friends at the big bus stop. They all have skateboards (5) ______________ we want to try some new tricks. It's great at the bus stop (6) ______________ we can meet more boys with skateboards there.

2 Schreibe die folgenden Zahlen als Worte auf.

1. 25 ______________ 2. 76 ______________

3. 68 ______________ 4. 44 ______________

3 Schreibe in einem Satz auf, wie spät es ist.

1. 12:00 ______________

2. 9:45 ______________

3. 5:15 ______________

4. 6:23 ______________

★ 4 Benutze ein Verbindungswort (z.B. and, so, but oder or) und ersetze Personen durch Pronomen.

1. Johnny wants to visit his grandma. Johnny leaves the house.

Johnny wants to visit his grandma, so he leaves the house.

2. It's Friday night. Becky and Tom are having a party.

____

3. Jenny wants to buy a new CD. Jenny hasn't got enough money.

____

5 Lies den Text und beantworte die Fragen. Schreibe die Zahlen oder Uhrzeiten aus.

It's 10:00 on Sunday morning. Jerry has got a competition at 12.30. They are 16 boys and girls in his team. At 13.15 Jerry has got his 1st race. Tom, his friend, has got a race at 2.45. It's his 14th race. Now it's Jerry's turn. Oh, he's 3rd and Tom is 9th. What a day!

1. What time is it on Sunday morning? __________
2. When is the competition? __________
3. How many boys and girls are in Jerry's team? __________
4. What happens at 1.15? __________
5. When is Tom's race? __________
6. It's Tom's __________ race today.
7. Tom and Jerry do not win the race. They are __________ and __________ .

6 Das Fahrradrennen. Ein Kommentator berichtet für das Radio, wie das Fahrradrennen ausgeht. Ergänze den Text:

Hello, my name is Jacky Fast and I'm live at the bike race in Stanton. The first bikes are arriving now:

1. Number *forty-five is first*
2. Number __________
3. __________ is __________
4. __________
5. __________

Anmerkung zum Umgang mit den Lösungen

1. Es gibt Übungen, bei denen du frei formulieren musst. Hier geben wir in der Lösung einen **Lösungsvorschlag** an, d.h. eine von mehreren Möglichkeiten, wie deine Lösung lauten könnte.
2. Achte bei diesen freien Übungen besonders auf die abgefragte Grammatik und die richtige Zeit.
3. Schaue erst in die Lösungen, wenn du alle Aufgaben eines Kapitels gelöst hast.
4. In den Lösungen der Tests findest du hinter der Aufgabennummer Hinweise, welches Thema du noch einmal üben solltest, falls du in einer Aufgabe Fehler gemacht hast.

Bestandsaufnahme

1 a) is, b) are (mehr dazu in Kapitel 1)
2 b) (mehr dazu in Kapitel 1)
3 c) (mehr dazu in Kapitel 1)
4 b) (mehr dazu in Kapitel 1)
5 1. c), 2. b), 3. c) (mehr dazu in Kapitel 3a)
6 a) (mehr dazu in Kapitel 3b)
7 1. c), 2. c) (mehr dazu in Kapitel 3b)
8 b) (mehr dazu in Kapitel 4a)
9 c) (mehr dazu in Kapitel 4b)
10 c) (mehr dazu in Kapitel 4a)
11 1. a), 2. b) (mehr dazu in Kapitel 3b)
12 1. b), 2. c) (mehr dazu in Kapitel 26 / 7a / 7b)
13 a), 2. b) (mehr dazu in Kapitel 19)
14 1. d), 2. a) (mehr dazu in Kapitel 11)
15 1. a), 2. a) (mehr dazu in Kapitel 20)
16 Last year I went to Australia *and* I visited my uncle Sam. My uncle was very happy to see me, *but* his dog wasn't happy. My aunt had dinner ready when we came home, *so* we sat down *and* had dinner. (mehr dazu in Kapitel 24)
17 1. b), 2. c) (mehr dazu in Kapitel 21)
18 1. c), 2. b) (mehr dazu in Kapitel 26)
19 c) (mehr dazu in Kapitel 22)

1 Formen von *to be*

1 I'm, is, I'm, are, are, what's, is, is

2 What's your name?

3
1. Is Mrs White your teacher?
2. Are they in your class?
3. Where are you from?
4. Who is in my room?

4 1. d), 2. c), 3. a), 4. b)

6 1. is, 2. are, 3. is, 4. are, 5. is, 6. am

7
1. Yes, I am. / No I'm not.
2. Yes, they are. / No, they aren't.
3. No, it isn't.
4. Yes, he / she is. No, he / she isn't.

Lösungen

8 1. Are you twelve? / Are you twelve years old?
2. Is Tim from England?
3. Are the girls at school?
4. Are you my new teacher?

9 2. He isn't in my class.
3. Zoe is from London.
4. Mr Old isn't my tutor at school.

10 1. Are you new here?
2. How old is Helen?

2a Personalpronomen

1 **Singular:** I, you, he, she, it; **Plural:** we, you, they

Das Personalpronomen you hat mehrere Bedeutungen. Es kann ihr, du, euch, Sie und Ihnen heißen.

2

Singular		Plural	
Langform	**Kurzform**	**Langform**	**Kurzform**
I am not	I'm not	we are not	we aren't
you are not	you aren't	you are not	you aren't
he is not	he isn't	they are not	they aren't
she is not	she isn't		
it is not	it isn't		

3 it und they

4 Lösungsvorschlag:
Is it a sweet cat? / Is it nice in your town?
Are they nice to you? / Are they all new in town?

5 Bitte achte auf die Groß- und Kleinschreibung der Wörter im Text.
Lösungswörter im Brief: Hello Jason / Helen, am, am, is, He, is, We, are, Are, am, I

6 Lösungsvorschlag:
Hello Whitney,
I'm Julia and I'm thirteen. My friend is Karen. She is from France. We are good friends. We aren't stars. But I am good at school, especially in English. I have got many friends at school. My English teacher is Mr Peterson. He is very nice.
Love, Julia ☺ ☺ ☺

7
1. She wants to meet him.
2. It sees it in the garden.
3. They like her.

8
Das Lösungswort lautet: PETS

2b Personalpronomen als Objekt

1

Akkusativ		Dativ		Nominativ	
Pete likes <u>me</u>.	mich	You can help <u>me.</u>	mir	I	ich
I like <u>you</u>.	dich / Sie	I can help <u>you.</u>	dir / Ihnen	you	du / Sie
We like <u>him.</u>	ihn	We can help <u>him.</u>	ihm	he	er
She likes <u>her.</u>	sie	I can help <u>her.</u>	ihr	she	sie
They like <u>it.</u>	es	You can help <u>it.</u>	ihm / ihr	it	es
He likes <u>us</u>.	uns	They can help <u>us.</u>	uns	we	wir
We like <u>you</u>.	euch / Sie	We can help <u>you.</u>	euch / Ihnen	you	ihr / Sie
We like <u>them</u>.	sie	They can help <u>them.</u>	ihnen	they	sie

2
2. sie, 3. ihm, 4. ihnen

3
2. ihn, 3. es

4
1) her, 2) them, 3) you, 4) us, 5) you, 6) him, 7) you

5
1. There is the cat. I can see it.
2. There's Tom's book. Bring him his book, please.
3. Can you help her, please?
4. Mary and Karen, can you help me, please?

6
2. She wants to meet him.
3. It sees it in the garden.
4. They like him.
5. He reads it.

Lösungen

Test 1

1. (Kapitel 1)
   1) is, 2) is, 3) are, 4) are, 5) is, 6) are

2. (Kapitel 2a)
   1. Sie ist ein nettes Mädchen.
   2. Sie sind coole Jungen.
   3. Sie ist im Garten.
   4. Sie sind in der Küche.

3. (Kapitel 2b)
   2. it, 3. him, 4. it, 5. her, 6. him, 7. them, 8. us

4. ★ (Kapitel 2a/2b)
   1) She, 2) she, 3) it, 4) him, 5) his, 6) her, 7) She, 8) They, 9) He

5. (Kapitel 1)
   1. Yes, he is. 2. No, she isn't. 3. No, they aren't. 4. Yes, it is. 5. No, it isn't. 6. No, I'm not. 7. Yes, I am. 8. No, you aren't.

6. (Kapitel 1)
   1. Are you from England?
   2. Are you at my school?
   3. Are you twelve, too?
   4. Where's the Tom-Hanson-School?
   5. Who is my teacher?

7. ★ (Kapitel 1)
   Lösungsvorschlag:
   1. Are you from London?
   2. Is your school very big?
   3. Are there nice girls in your class?
   4. Are you a big family?
   5. Is there a cinema in your town?

3a *Simple present*

1 Wir benutzen das simple present, wenn etwas regelmäßig oder oft geschieht, z.B. jeden Tag. Merke dir Signalwörter: every (day / morning / week / year etc.), always, sometimes, often

2 Die Verneinung bildet man mit don't oder doesn't und dem Infinitv. Man benutzt doesn't nur bei he / she / it.

3 Lösungsvorschlag:
2. I have breakfast at 7.15.
3. I do my homework at 3 o'clock.
4. I go to bed at 8 o'clock.

4
2. Johnny and Swimmy don't eat fish sandwiches.
3. The pupils in year 5 don't have a computer in their classroom.
4. My dad doesn't drive a motorbike. / My dad drives a motorbike.

5
2. Jane and Sam play tennis but they don't play basketball.
3. Tom goes to school by skateboard but he doesn't go by bus.
4. My grandma likes cats but she doesn't like frogs.

3b *Simple present* – **Fragen**

1
1. Do you like the new player in the football team? Yes, I do.
2. Where do you usually play? We play behind the school on the field.
3. And where do you play football? I don't play football very often.
4. Do you have a good ball? Yes, I do.

2 1. Yes, I do. 2. No, they don't. 3. Yes, he does.

4 1. d), 2. e), 3. b), 4 c), 5 a)

Merke: Im simple present werden Fragen mit Vollverben so gebildet: do oder does + Subjekt + Infintiv. Fragewörter wie z.B. when, where, what werden vor das do oder does gestellt.

5 1. when, 2. do, 3. do, 4. what do, 5. when do, 6. does, 7. do, 8. when do

6
1. Does she drink coke every day?
2. When does the bus arrive at the station?
3. Does your friend like the new CD?
4. Where does the new boy in our class live?

7 Lösungsvorschlag:
1. I live in Düsseldorf.
2. No, she doesn't. / Yes, she does.
3. I often play outside in the afternoon.
4. Yes, they do.
5. I often have a toast and a glass of milk.
6. Yes, they do. / No, they don't.

4a *Present progressive*

2
2. The woman is reading.
3. The girl is swimming.
4. The boys are drawing.

Form von to be + Grundform + ing-Form
Signalwörter: at the moment, now, right now

3 a) Die ing-Form wird an die Grundform des Verbs angehängt. b) Das ‚e' am Ende des Wortes fällt weg und die ing-Form wird angehängt. c) Endet das Verb in der Grundform auf m, n, t, wird der Konsonant verdoppelt und die ing-Form angehängt.

4
1. A boy is cleaning the board.
2. A girl is reading a book.
3. A boy is opening / closing the window.
4. Two girls are playing a game.
5. A boy is eating a sandwich.
6. A girl is writing into her exercise book.

5
1. Two girls are eating a pizza.
2. One boy is playing tennis.
3. Two boys are going by bike.
4. Lösungsvorschlag: Dad / A man is driving a car / by car.

4b *Present progressive*-Fragen

1

2. No, they aren't.
3. No, she isn't.
4. Yes, she is.
5. Yes, they are.

2

Man bildet eine Frage im present progressive mit einer Form von <u>to be</u> (is, am oder are) + Subjekt + ing- Form

3

1. Are you learning English?
2. Is the dog playing in the garden?

4

Achte beim Einsetzen auf die Groß- und Kleinschreibung.

1. Is, 2. Is, going, 3. visiting, 4. Where, are, 5. the cat, 6. Are, writing

5

2. No, it isn't. It's reading a book.
3. No, it isn't. It's drinking coffee.
4. No, they aren't. They're playing football.
5. No, it isn't. It's eating a flower.

6

Lösungsvorschlag:

2. Is he drawing a picture?
3. Is she buying a new CD?
4. Am I washing the car?
5. Are they sleeping on the sofa?
6. Is he talking to a friend?

Lösungen

5 *Simple present* und *present progressive* im Vergleich

1
Signalwörter simple present: often, always, never, sometimes, usually, every week / year / month,
Signalwörter present progressive: at the moment, now, right now

3
1. often / sometimes
2. often / sometimes
3. at the moment / right now / now
4. at the moment / right now / now

4
1. at the moment- are swimming
2. every Sunday- go
3. on Mondays- eats
4. sometimes- plays
5. never- talk
6. at the moment- is cleaning
7. often- ride
8. isn't baking- at the moment

5
2. Sam and his father often go swimming on Saturday morning. This Saturday they are playing basketball.
3. Mary sometimes goes shopping with her mother on Fridays. This Friday they are baking a cake.
4. Mum usually listens to the news in the morning. This morning she is watching the news on TV.

Test 2

1
(Kapitel 3a)
1. Every Monday they go to school. / They go to school every Monday.
2. Every Tuesday he watches TV with his dad. / He watches TV with his dad every Tuesday.
3. Every week they play hockey at school. / They play hockey at school every week.
4. The cat eats a mouse every month. / Every month the cat eats a mouse.

2
(Kapitel 3a / 4a / 5)
2. ~~jump-~~ are jumping
3. ~~is eating-~~ eats
4. Der Satz ist richtig.
5. ~~is buying-~~ buys

3
(Kapitel 3a / 4a / 5)
1. sees
2. are reading
3. go
4. drinks
5. is running

4 (Kapitel 3b / 4b)
1. What are you doing at the moment?
2. Where do you play football on Mondays?

5 (Kapitel 3b / 4b)
1. Yes, she does.
2. No, he isn't.
3. No, they aren't.
4. No, it doesn't.
5. No, she isn't.
6. Yes, they do.
7. Yes, we do.
8. Yes, I am./Yes, we are.

6 (Kapitel 3b / 4b)
Lösungsvorschlag:
1. He goes to school at 7.30 on Tuesdays.
2. They are reading a book.
3. We go to France every summer.
4. I usually listen to music in the afternoon.

7 (Kapitel 3b / 4b)
Lösungsvorschlag:
1. What is your favourite sport?
2. What does Peter do on Tuesdays? / When does Peter play basketball?
3. What are Jane and Olivia doing at the moment? / Who is doing their homework?

6 Unregelmäßige Verben

1 To play ist ein regelmäßiges Verb, man hängt im simple past ein -ed an. To do und to buy sind unregelmäßige Verben. Die simple past Formen muss man lernen.

2 to do- did
to go- went
to have- had
to come- came
to make- made
to see- saw
to run- ran

3 1. was-be, 2. lived-live, 3. had-have, 4. went-go, 5. met-meet, 6. lived-live 7. didn't like-not like, 8. invited-invite, 9. said-say, 10. became-become, 11. put-put, 12. lived-live, 13. died-die

4 1. went, 2. put, 3. ate, 4. won

5 1) was, 2) put, 3) spoke, 4) didn't have, 5) took, 6) was, 7) saw, 8) was, 9) said, 10) sat, 11) was, 12) saw, 13) was, 14) gave, 15) went, 16) said, 17) took, 18) showed

6 Lösungsvorschlag:
1. Yesterday I took the dog for a walk in the park.
2. Last Monday I saw my best friend at his house.

7a *Simple past*

1 1. was, 2. were, 3. was, 4. were

2 1. Gestern spielte ich mit meinem besten Freund.
2. Letzten Samstag war ich im Kino.

Das simple past benutzt man, wenn man erzählt, was in der Vergangenheit passierte. Es gibt folgende Signalwörter: yesterday, last month, two weeks ago, in 2004 Regelmäßige Verben enden im simple past auf – ed. Unregelmäßige Verben haben keine Regel für ihre Bildung, man muss sie einfach lernen. (mehr dazu in Kapitel 6 und auf S. 126)

3 Im simple past werden Vollverben mit didn't + Infinitiv verneint. Diese Regel gilt für alle Personen. Die verneinten simple past Formen von to be heißen wasn't (Singular) und weren't (Plural).

4 1. was, 2. saw, 3. came, 4. saw, was, 5. looked, 6. landed, 7. came, 8. said, 9. was, had, 10. gave, 11. filled, flew, 12. was

5 1. two years ago-was
2. last weekend-came
3.yesterday-gave
4. Last Monday-went
5. last night-watched
6. Yesterday-cleaned

6 1. didn't go, 2. rode, 3. didn't get, 4. slept, 5. wasn't, 6. didn't like

7b *Simple past*- Fragen

1 1. b), 2. a), 3. d), 4. c), 5. f), 6. e)

2 Did you see them again?

3 Lösungsvorschlag:
1. When did he / she / they leave?
2. Who bought the bag for you?
3. Which bag did you carry?
4. Where did he / she / they go?
5. What did he / she / they do?

4
1. yesterday-did
2. last month-where
3. last Sunday-who
4. last week-did buy
5. kein Signalwort-who took

5
1.c) Yes, she did.
2.e) She met him in the library.
3.f) She bought the new CD of Tokio Hotel.
4.b) Jason wrote an A.
5.d) No, they didn't.
6.a) They went at 7 o'clock.

6 Lösungsvorschlag:
1. Did you swim in the sea?
2. Did you stay at / sleep in a hotel?
3. Did you meet nice girls?
4. Did you visit / see a castle?
5. Did you buy a souvenir?

Test 3

1 (Kapitel 7a)
1. went, 2. were, 3. visited, 4. ran, 5. didn't do, 6. bought, 7. didn't like,
8. didn't eat-ate-cooked

2 (Kapitel 7b)
1. Did he play the piano this afternoon?
2. When did they leave the house?
3. Which book did she want for her birthday?
4. Where did you stay on the class trip?

3 (Kapitel 7b)
1. Yes, we / I did. 2. No, he didn't. 3. No, they didn't. 4. Yes, I did. 5. Yes, she did.
6. No, we / I didn't.

4 (Kapitel 7b)
Lösungsvorschlag:
1. I met him at 8 o'clock.
2. She liked him because he was so funny.
3. We wrote a Maths test.
4. It was my uncle Fred.
5. I put it into the kitchen.

5 (Kapitel 7b)
Lösungsvorschlag:
1. Did you really saw Brad Pitt in the hotel?
2. Who was the woman in the shop?
3. When did you leave in the morning?
4. Where did you sleep / stay last weekend?

6 (Kapitel 6 / 7a)
Die unregelmäßigen Verben aus dem Rätsel sind unterstrichen.
see- saw, have- had, be- was, buy- bought, hurt- hurt, drink- drank, go- went, do- did, say- said, sit- sat, take- took, come- came

8 Wortstellung in Aussagesätzen

4 Im simple present Satz stehen Adverbien zwischen dem Subjekt und dem Verb.

6
1. The pupils are sitting in the bus.
2. Sarah and I have got a pink bikes.
3. Mr Brown sometimes goes swimming on Saturdays.
4. They often play games in the evening.
5. We meet the nice girls at the pool every Monday.

7 1. always / never / often, 2. never, 3. nice / clever, 4. always / never / often, 5. quick / nice, 6. nice / clever

8 Die Botschaft lautet: *I meet you in the cafeteria at 8 o'clock.*

9 Fragewörter

1 2. where- wo 3. when- wann 4. how many- wie viele 5. why- warum 6. who- wer 7. which- welche/s

3 1b. Wo ist deine Schule?
2a. Where are my friends?
3b. Wer ist der Mann?
4a. Who is the new boy?
Verwechsle nicht who und where, denn who heißt im Deutschen wer und where bedeutet wo.

4 1.when 2. where- who 3. where 4. where 5. where- which 6. where- which 7. who 8. why 9. why 10. why- when 11. what 12. when- why 13. who 14. who

5 1. Where is your book?
2. How are you?
3. When is your birthday ?
4. Where is your brother?
5. Which/What is your favourite song?

6 1. When is the meeting at the bus stop? When is the meeting at the shop? When do they meet? What is at the bus stop? What is on the bus? What is a bus / shop / bus stop?
2. Where is he / she from? Who is he / she? Where is he / she?
3. Who are the girls in the corner? How are the girls?
4. Why are the dogs in the garden? Why is the dog in the garden?

Lösungen

10 Fragen und ihre Antworten

1

1. present progressive
2. simple present
3. simple past
4. simple present
5. present progressive

2

TIPP: Hast du darauf geachtet, in welcher Zeit die Frage steht? Dann findest du die Antwort einfacher.

1. b), 2. c), 3. a), 4. d), 5. g), 6. e), 7. h), 8. f)

3

Lösungsvorschlag:
1. No, they aren't. / Yes, they are.
2. Yes, she does. / No, she doesn't.
3. No he/she didn't. / Yes, he/she did.
4. Yes, I do. / No, I don't.
5. We talk too much during the lessons. I am not sitting next to him because we are too loud when we are together.
6. I learnt / learned for it yesterday. / Yesterday I studied for it.

TIPP: Wenn du auf eine Frage antwortest, überlege zuerst, in welcher Zeit die Frage steht und schreibe dann die Antwort auf. Manchmal helfen dir Signalwörter.

4

1. Yes, they did.
2. No, I don't.
3. Yes, it does.
4. No, she didn't.

5

Lösungsvorschlag:
1. I went swimming in the new pool.
2. Yes, they have. / No, they haven't.
3. Maths is my favourite subject.
4. Yes, I do. / No, I don't.
5. I live in Munich.
6. No, I'm not. I'm sitting on my bed. / Yes, I am.

6

Lösungsvorschlag:
2. What are your hobbies?
3. When do you go to school on Tuesdays / every Tuesday?
4. Who has got a flat with a balcony?
5. Why do you want to go out?
6. Where are Peter and Karl going?

11 Präpositionen

1 Präpositionen im Text: on, under, in, next to, behind, under, in front of

2 1. under – unter, 2. next to – neben, 3. in – in, 4. in front of – vor, 5. behind - hinter, 6. on – auf

3 2. The book is under the bag.
3. The book is behind the bag.
4. The is next to the bag.
5. The book is in front of the bag.
6. The book is on the bag.

4 Lösungsvorschlag:
1. There is pencil case on the desk.
2. There are pens in the pencil case.
3. There is a rubber on the desk.
4. There is a ruler on the desk.
5. There are three books on the table.
6. There is a school bag on the chair.
7. There is a mouse under the bed.
8. There is a comic / magazine on the bed.
9. There is a skateboard on the floor.
10. There is a cat behind the window.
11. There are CDs on the floor.
12. There is a football under the desk.
13. There is a poster on the wall.

5 Lösungsvorschlag:
1. My teacher is under the desk.
2. My best friend is in the cupboard.
3. My parents are behind my school bag.
4. My mother is under my bed.
5. My best friend is next to the pond.

6 2. No, it isn't. It's <u>on</u> the bed.
3. No, they aren't. They are <u>under</u> the table.
4. No, it isn't. It's <u>in</u> its basket. / It's <u>in</u> a basket.

Lösungen

Test 4

1 (Kapitel 8)
1. He reads a book.
2. Our German teacher doesn't speak English.
3. Peter and John are making sandwiches.
4. I didn't understand the text.
5. The cat always drinks milk.
6. Karen doesn't like the new German teacher.

2 (Kapitel 9)
1. where-when-why, 2. which, 3. where, 4. what-how, 5. where-how, 6. why, 7. where-who-which, 8. where-why-when, 9. where, 10. what

3 (Kapitel 10)
Lösungsvorschlag:
1. Yes, I did. / No, I didn't.
2. Yes, they are. / No, they aren't.
3. I want to visit you on Saturday.
4. Yes, she does. / No, she doesn't.
5. She is going to the bike shop.
6. Yes, you can. / No, you can't.

4 TIPP Wenn du über etwas aus der Vergangenheit sprechen willst, musst du das simple past benutzen.

(Kapitel 10)
Lösungsvorschlag:
1. What did you do on your last day in the USA?
2. Where did you stay?
3. When did your plane leave?
4. What was your favourite food in the USA?
5. Why didn't you write a postcard?
6. Who is the girl in the picture? / Who was with you in the plane?

5 (Kapitel 11)
1. on the desk
2. in the kitchen
3. under the chair
4. next to the shelf
5. behind the door
6. in the bedroom
7. in front of the house
8. in front of the cinema

6 TIPP Bei dieser Reportage musst du das present progressive benutzen, denn der Reporter beschreibt live, wer was macht.

(Kapitel 8)
1. John is running 50 metres.
2. Helen and Tom are jumping.
3. Jane is throwing balls.
4. The coach is shouting at the athletes.

7 (Kapitel 9 / 10)
Lösungsvorschlag:
1. What did you read at school last month?
2. When do Susan and Helen go with the dog for a walk?
3. What are the dogs doing?
4. How are you?
5. Where can we watch the new Mr Bean film?

12a *Can / can't*

2 b)

Can ist ein Hilfsverb und kann nie alleine stehen, es braucht immer noch ein Vollverb. Nach can steht immer der Infintiv.

3 Auch nach can't / cannot steht immer der Infinitiv.

4
2. They can write in English.
3. We can swim in the sea.
4. You can't speak in the Maths lesson.

3 1. can't play, 2. can sing, 3. can help, 4. can't run

6 Lösungsvorschlag:
1. A dog can play with me.
2. Mum and Dad can help me in the garden.
3. My cousin can speak Spanish.
4. My cousin can't play the piano.
5. Tracy can't read a book in French.
6. A dog can't read a book.

7
2. Mary can go by bike, but she can't drive a car.
3. Tony and Helen can play badminton, but they can't play tennis.
4. The pupils can't write on a paper, but they can write in exercise books.

12b *Can you ...?*- Fragen mit *can*

1. Can you help me with my bike, Dad? – Yes, I can.
Can Kim and Jill bake a cake for Grandma? – No, they can't.
Can I play at the computer, Mum? – No, you can't.
Can Jason play the piano? – Yes, he can.

2. Im Aussagesatz steht can nach dem Subjekt des Satzes. Bei Fragen, wird can vor das Subjekt des Satzes gestellt. Bei Fragen mit Fragewörtern, steht can zwischen dem Fragewort und dem Subjekt des Satzes.

3.
1. Can the cat sleep in your bed?
2. Can Mr Grease be nice, too?
3. Can you open the window, please?
4. Can Sandra come to the cinema with us?

4.
1. Can she / you dance with me?
2. Can you / they be nice? / Can you / they be nice to Jenny? / Can you be nice to your sister Jenny? / Can they be nice to your sister Jenny? Can you be nice to your sister, Jenny? / Can they be nice to your sister, Jenny?
(Achtung, mit einem Komma vor dem Wort Jenny bekommen zwei Fragen eine andere Bedeutung.)
3. Can they / he play in the garden?
4. Can he sit next to me?

5. Lösungsvorschlag:
1. No, I can't. / Yes, I can.
2. No, they can't.
3. No, she can't. / Yes, she can.
4. Yes, they can. / No, they can't.

6. Lösungsvorschlag:
1. Can you drive a car?
2. Can you play a computer game with me?
3. Can you repair a bike?
4. Can you sing a song for me?

13 *Must / mustn't / needn't*

1

1. You must be quiet.
2. They mustn't shout.
3. We must read a book.
4. He needn't do a test.
5. She mustn't play outside.

Die Übersetzung von must ist müssen, mustn't heißt nicht dürfen, und needn't bedeutet nicht müssen oder nicht brauchen. Nach must / mustn't oder needn't folgt immer ein Infintiv.

2

1. Ihr müsst um 9 Uhr im Bett sein.
2. Ihr dürft kein Handy mitbringen.
3. Ihr braucht nicht um 6 Uhr aufzustehen, aber ihr müsst um 7.30 Uhr aufstehen.
4. Eure Eltern müssen zum Treffen in der Schule am Freitag Nachmittag kommen.

3

1. mustn't, 2. must, 3. must, 4. needn't

4

Lösungsvorschlag:
2. You mustn't turn left here.
3. You mustn't eat ice cream here.
4. You must stop here.
5. You mustn't use your mobile phone here.

5

2. It's cold outside: They mustn't wear a summer jacket.
3. It's hot outside: The pupils needn't do their homework.
4. It's raining outside. Peter and Tim must take an umbrella.

14 *a / an – the*

1

Der unbestimmte Artikel a / an heißt im Deutschen: ein, eine. Man benutzt a, wenn das folgende Wort mit einem **gesprochenen** Konsonanten beginnt. Man benutzt an, wenn das folgende Wort mit einem **gesprochenen** Vokal beginnt.

2

1. die beste Pizza, 2. das Mädchen aus England, 3. der alte Mann von nebenan

In der englischen Sprache gibt es nur **einen** bestimmten Artikel, und zwar für Singular und für Plural: the. In der deutschen Sprache gibt es drei Artikel: der, die und das.

4

[ðə]		[ðiː]	
chair	car	orange	apple
guitar	bike	afternoon	exercise
unit	board	end	idea

5 1. [ði:] 2. [ðə] 3. [ði:] 4. [ðə] 5. [ðə]

6 1. a, 2. an, 3. a / a, 4. an, 5. a, 6. an / a

7 Wir wissen nicht, was du in deiner Tasche hast. Daher haben wir ein paar Möglichkeiten überlegt. Lösungsvorschlag: 2) an apple, 3) a pencil case, 4) an English book, 5) a German book, 6) a calculator, 7) a ruler, 8) a folder, 9) a banana, 10) a lunchbox, 11) a dictionary, 12) a bar of chocolate, 13) a sandwich, 14) a favourite book, 15) a key, 16) an orange, 17) a pen, 18) an orange folder, 19) a vocabulary book, 20) an English test

15 *have got / has got*

2

Singular	Plural
Kurzform	Kurzform
I**'ve got** a computer. You**'ve got** a sweet cat.	We**'ve got** You**'ve got** They**'ve got** a mobile.

3 You **haven't got** a sweet cat.
He **hasn't got** a black cap.
She **hasn't got** a black cap.
It **hasn't got** a black basket.

We / You / They → **haven't got** a mobile.

Es gibt zwei Formen von have got: have got und has got. Die Verneinung lautet: haven't got / hasn't got. In Fragen wird das Hilfsverb have vor das Subjekt gestellt.

4 2. Has, 3. Have we got, 4. Has she got, 5. Have they got, 6. Have I got

5 Lösungsvorschlag:
2. Have your friends got a dog? Yes, they have. / No, they haven't.
3. Has your mother got a car? Yes, she has. / No, she hasn't.

6 1. The pigs haven't got a ball.
2. The cat hasn't got a computer.
3. The horse hasn't got a school bag.
4. The cow hasn't got a bike.

★7 1. Has Tilo got a dog?
2. Have you got a friend?
3. Mum and Dad, have you got time?
4. Has Nina got the new CD?

16 *Would like to* und *want to*

1. Es ist unhöflich I want to in einem Restaurant zu sagen.

Man benutzt would like to, wenn man höflich sein will. I would like to bedeutet ich möchte gerne und I want to bedeutet ich will.

2. Waiter: What would you like to drink?
Jason: I want to drink a large coke!
Mrs Ken: Jason, that's not polite. Order again, please.
Jason: I would like to have a large coke, please. Is that OK, Mum?

Nach would like to und want to steht immer der Infintiv des Verbs. Bei he / she / it braucht want , ein –s, would bleibt unverändert.

3. 1. c), 2. b), 3. d), 4. a)

4. Lösungsvorschlag:
1. Peter and Tom want to play a game.
2. Mrs Johnson would like to read the new book.
3. The cat wants to catch a mouse.
4. Conny would like to dance with Tom.

5. 1. would like to, 2. want to, 3. wants to oder auch would like to, 4. would like to

6. 1. What would you like to drink?
2. Jason would like to have a new bike.
3. I would like to eat fish and chips.

Lösungen

Test 5

1 (Kapitel 12a / 12b)
1. can't write, 2. can jump, 3. can't sing, 4. can you give, 5. can you be

2 (Kapitel 13)
2. You mustn't shout at me.
3. You must knock at the door.
4. You needn't bring chocolate.
5. Parents must be nice in my room.

3 (Kapitel 13)
1. must, 2. mustn't, 3. needn't, 4. must

4 (Kapitel 14)
1) a, 2) an, 3) a, 4) a, 5) an, 6) a, 7) an

5 (Kapitel 14)
[ðə]: pencil case, book, table, unit, chair, girl
[ðiː]: old pencil case, apple, exercise book, English girl

6 (Kapitel 14)
a: boy, toast, unit
an: egg, ice cream, orange

7 (Kapitel 15)
Lösungsvorschlag:
1. Yes, I have. / No, I haven't.
2. Yes, he has. / No, he hasn't.
3. Have you got a new bike?
4. Has Jane got a new dog?

8 (Kapitel 18)
2. Mum, I want to play football with my friends.
3. Hello, I would like to book a room in your hotel, please.

17 Singular – Plural

1 Hinweis: Die zugeordneten Paare findest du unten in der Tabelle in der Lösung für Aufgabe 2.

Lösungsvorschlag:
1. Man bildet die Pluralform, indem ein -s angehängt wird. Beispiel: dog-dogs
2. Aus einem -y am Ende wird –ies. Beispiel: cherry-cherries
3. Es wird ein ganz neues Wort gebildet. Beispiel: mouse-mice
4. Das Wort hat im Singular und im Plural die gleiche Form. Beispiel: fish-fish

2

regelmäßig + s	unregelmäßig (neues Wort)	y → ies	Konsonant (s,ch,x) + es	Singular =Plural
bike – bikes	mouse – mice	cherry – cherries	sandwich – sandwiches	fish = fish
dog – dogs	child – children	ferry – ferries	box – boxes	sheep = sheep
table – tables	foot – feet	country – countries	class – classes	
postcard – postcards	woman – women			

3 1. fish, 2. cats, 3. children, 4. sheep, 5. mice, 6. feet, 7. CDs, 8. countries

4 Hinweis: Die erste Form ist die Singularform.
1. sheep – sheep, 2. cake – cakes, 3. biscuit – biscuits, 4. baby – babies, 5. church – churches, 6. eye – eyes, 7. family – families, 8. lemonade – lemonades / bottle – bottles

5 1. eleven old women **oder** eleven old ladies, 2. eight young families, 3. three nice neighbours

18 *There is – there are*

1 Hinweis: Achte darauf, dass man am Anfang eines Satzes in den Übungen groß schreibt.
3. there is, 4. there is, 5. there is, 6. there are, 7. there is, 8. there are, 9. there is, 10. there are

Mit there is / there are kann man auf Personen oder Dinge hinweisen.
Im Singular benutzt man there is oder kurz there's: Im Plural benutzt man there are.
Im Deutschen sagt man **es gibt** oder **(es) ist** oder **(es) sind**.

2 1. ist, 2. sind, 3. Es gibt / Dort sind

3 Hinweis: Achte darauf, dass am Anfang des Satzes groß geschrieben wird.
1. there are, 2. there are, 3. there is, 4. there is, 5. there are, 6. there are, 7. there is, 8. there are

4
2. There are six sheep on my farm.
3. There is one cat on my farm. / There's a cat on my farm.
4. There is one dog on my farm. / There's a dog on my farm.
5. There are three geese on my farm.
6. There are two rabbits on my farm.
7. There are ten chickens on my farm.

5 Lösungsvorschlag:
Hinweis: Bei dieser Aufgabe gibt es natürlich viele Varianten. Daher findest du hier nur einige Möglichkeiten.
2. There is an old piece of cheese under the bed.
3. There are ten comics on the floor.
4. There is a dirty plate on a chair.

19 *Much – many / some – any*

1 1. c), 2. d), 3. a), 4. b)

Much steht vor <u>nicht zählbaren Substantiven</u>, und many steht vor <u>zählbaren Substantiven</u>. Beide werden hauptsächlich in Fragen und verneinten Sätzen benutzt. In bejahten Sätzen ird dagegen meistens a lot of oder lots of benutzt.

2 1. much, 2. much, 3. many, 4. many

3 1. many, 2. many, 3. lots of, a lot of, 4. a lot of

4 1. viele Freunde, 2. viel Geld, 3. viele Schweine, 4. viel Zucker

5 1. a lot of / lots of toys, 2. many animals, 3. a lot of / much tea, 4. much money, 5. much left, 6. many cats

6 Lösungsvorschlag:
1. How much is a comic?
2. How many Batman comics have you got?
3. How many comics do you want to buy / to have?
4. How much money have you got?

20 *this – that / these – those*

1 1. d), 2. a), 3. b), 4. c)

Man benutzt this und these für Dinge, die in der Nähe sind.
Man benutzt that und those für Dinge, die weiter entfernt sind.

2 Achte bei deinen Lösungen auf die Groß- und Kleinschreibung!
1. these, 2. this, 3. that, 4. here, 5. over there, 6. here, 7. this, 8. that

3 1. this, those, 2. that

4 Achte bei deinen Lösungen auf die Groß- und Kleinschreibung!
1. these, 2. that, 3. this, 4. those, 5. this, those

5 2. these, 3. this, 4. that, 5. those, 6. those, this

21 *s*-Genitiv und *of*-Genitiv

1 Der s-Genitiv zeigt die Zugehörigkeit zu Personen und Tieren an. Das bedeutet, dass man den s-Genitiv immer dann benutzt, wenn etwas zu einer Person oder zu einem Tier gehört.

2 Der Satz lautet: *These are the girls' pullovers.*

3 Der s-Genitiv gilt auch bei Pluralformen, die auf -s enden. In solchen Fällen wird nach dem –s nur noch ein Apostroph angehängt.

4 1. table, 2. house, 3. street, 4. T- shirts

Der of-Genitiv dagegen zeigt die Zugehörigkeit zu Sachen und Gegenständen an, im Singular und im Plural.

5 1. Peter's cat, 2. boys' skateboards, 3. neighbours' dogs , 4. cat's toy
5. girls' hamster, 6. Jason's books, 7. dog's biscuits, 8. teacher's desk, 9. boys' room ,
10. children's lunchboxes

6 2. These are the teachers of our school.
3. This is the garden of our house.
4. These are the books of the old library.

★7 TIPP Achte bei deinen Lösungen insbesondere auf die richtig Anzahl in den einzelnen Aussagen.

2. der Freund meiner Brüder, 3. die Freunde meiner Brüder, 4. die Freunde meines Bruders, 5. der Korb der Hunde, 6. die Körbe des Hundes, 7. die Körbe der Hunde, 8. der Korb des Hundes

22 Possessivbegleiter

1 1. deine, 2. mein, 3. unser, 4. ihre, 5. sein

Die Possessivbegleiter zeigen an, wem etwas gehört.

2 Its bedeutet sein(e) / ihr(e). It's besteht aus it und is. Es bedeutet er / sie / es ist. Your bedeutet dein(e) / euer / Ihr(e). You're besteht aus you und are. Es bedeutet du bist / ihr seid / Sie sind.

3

Englisch		Deutsch	
I	my	ich	mein / meine
you	your	du / Sie	dein/deine, Ihr/Ihre
he	his	er	sein / seine
she	her	sie	ihr / ihre
it	its	es	sein / seine
we	our	wir	unser/unsere
you	your	ihr / Sie	euer / eure, Ihr / Ihre
they	their	sie (Pl.)	ihr / ihre

4 1. my, your, 2. our, 3. my, 4. their

5 Hinweis: Achte auf die Groß- und Kleinschreibung.
1. they're, their, 2. its, 3. it's, 4. you're, your

6 1. their, 2. his, 3. its, 4. their, 5. your

7 1. Can you show me your house?
2. Can you give me your pencils?
3. Is this your dog?

23 Aufforderungen und Verbote

1 Imperative im Dialog

Sam: Jenny, come here.
Jenny: Yes, what's wrong?
Sam: Clean the kitchen before Mum comes home.
Jenny: OK.
Sam: Jenny, get me a hot chocolate.
Jenny: Just a minute.
Sam: Jenny, bake a cake for us.
Jenny: AHHHHHHHH, Sam, I'm not your slave! Shut your big mouth or ...
Sam: OK, it was only a joke.

2 Der Imperativ wird mit dem Infintiv des Verbs gebildet.

3 Lösungsvorschlag:
1. Hey Thomas, clean my bike. / Clean my bike.
2. Clean up my room, Theresa. / Tidy up my room.

4 Der verneinte Imperativ (Verbot) wird mit don't und dem Infintiv gebildet.

5
1. Go to your room.
2. Bring them two cups of coffee.
3. Clean our budgie's cage.

6
3. Don't get up too late.
4. Close the window.
5. Do your homework.
6. Don't throw the ball in the house.

7 Lösungsvorschlag:
1. Don't turn left.
2. Don't talk here. / Be quiet.
3. Don't swim here.
4. Don't play with the ball here.
5. Wear a helmet.
6. Wash your hands.

Lösungen

Test 6

1 (Kapitel 17)
1) sandwiches, 2) balls, 3) children, 4) ferries, 5) sheep, 6) mice, 7) cats, 8) rulers, 9) fish

2 (Kapitel 18)
1) there are, 2) there is, 3) there are, 4) there is, 5) there are, 6) there is, 7) there are

3 (Kapitel 19)
1. much, a lot of, 2. much, a lot of, 3. many, a lot of, 4. a lot of, a lot of, 5. much, a lot of

4 (Kapitel 20)
1. These CDs here are my favourite CDs.
2. That CD over there is cool, too.
3. Those girls and boys over there are really nice.

5 (Kapitel 21)
1. This is Peter's book.
2. The colour of the house is green.
3. This is the neighbours' car.
4. Vorsicht! Denke daran, dass man bei Tieren den s-Genitiv braucht.The cat's basket is brown.

6 (Kapitel 22)
Hinweis: Achte auf die Groß- und Kleinschreibung.
1. their, 2. its, 3. her, 4. our

24 Verbindungswörter

1 1. The little rabbit Carl is in his house <u>and</u> is eating lunch. Someone is knocking at the door, <u>so</u> he opens it. It's his friend, the little hedgehog Sammy. They want to do something. Carl and Sammy don't want to go swimming <u>because</u> it's boring. The two friends don't want to work in the house <u>or</u> in the garden. They want to have a little party with their friends Tilly, the fox <u>and</u> Otto, the mouse.

2. Lösungsvorschlag:
Der zweite Text hört sich besser an und ist abwechslungsreicher formuliert.

2 1) und, 2) aber, 3) also / deswegen, 4) weil, 5) oder

3 1. and, 2. so, 3. but / and, 4. or, 5. because

4 2. Jenny and Tom like English but they don't like Geography.
3. Tim reads comics but he doesn't read books about Germany.
4. Cats eat mice but frogs don't like them.

5 1. She plays computer games every afternoon but she doesn't play at night.
2. Peter eats pizza and he also eats hamburgers with a lot of cheese.

6 Lösungsvorschlag:
Hinweis: Die Lösungen geben nur eine von vielen Möglichkeiten an.
1. My family likes family games because they can be so funny.
2. I can jump into the water or swim in the sea.
3. It's very nice outside, so let's play in the park.

25 Zahlen bis 100 – Ordnungszahlen

1 2. thirteen, 3. fifty-six, 4. one, 6. seventy-five, 7. three, 8. thirty, 9. eighty-eight, 10. twelve, 11. forty, 12. ninety- nine

2 1) third, 2) fourth, 3) fifth

1., 2., 3. heißen im Englischen: first, second, third.

3 "oh-double two-one-three-one-two-three-four-double five-eight-nine"

4

3. – third	13th – thirteenth
17 – seventeen	22. – twenty-second
30. – thirtieth	31 – thirty-one
47– forty- seven	54 – fifty- four

5 1. 36, 2. 60, 3. 12, 4. 17, 5. 14, 6. 45, 7. 20, 8. 87, 9. 93

6 1. nineteen, 2. thirteen, 3. fifteen, 4 twenty-five, 5. seventy-eight , 6. ninety-nine, 7. sixty-seven, 8. eighty-one

7 1. Jane, 2. Tim, 3. Helen, 4. John

26 Die Uhrzeit

1 1. d), 2. a) ,3. b) ,4. c), 5. e)

Bei Uhrzeiten zwischen voller und halber Stunde benutzt man: past.
Bei Uhrzeiten zwischen halber und voller Stunde benutzt man to.
Den Begriff o'clock benutzt man nur bei vollen Stunden.
Quarter to heißt Viertel vor, quarter past heißt Viertel nach.
Bei Minuten zwischen den Fünferschritten muss man zusätzlich minutes sagen.

2 1. b), 2. f); 3. c); 4. e); 5. d), 6. h), 7. a), 8. g)

3
1. 6:15 oder 18:15,
2. 3:24 oder 15:24
3. 7:30 oder 19:30
4. 10:34 oder 22:34
5. 7:55 oder 19:55
6. 12:00 oder 00:00
7. 8:45 oder 20:45
8. 11:19 oder 23:19

4
1. It's seven- thirty ~~o'clock~~. It's half past seven.
Oder der Bindestrich und o'clock werden weggestrichen und es heißt: It's seven thirty.
2. It's half past ~~five~~. It's half past four.
3. It's twenty-five ~~past~~ two. It's twenty- five to two.
4. It's quarter ~~to~~ nine. It's quarter past nine.

5
2. It's quarter to ten. 9:45 oder 21:45
3. It's twenty- five past twelve. 12:25 oder 00:25
4. It's half past six. 6:30 oder 18:30
5. It's quarter past eight. 8:15 oder 20:15

Test 7

1 (Kapitel 24)
1) and, 2) and / so, 3) but, 4) and, 5) so / and. 6) because / and

2 (Kapitel 25)
1. twenty-five, 2. seventy-six, 3. sixty-eight, 4. forty-four

3 (Kapitel 26)
1. It's twelve o'clock.
2. It's quarter to ten.
3. It's quarter past five.
4. It's twenty-three minutes past six.

4 (Kapitel 24)
1. It's Friday night and / so Becky and Tom are having a party.
2. Jenny wants to buy a new CD, but she hasn't got enough money.

5 (Kapitel 25 / 26)
1. It's ten o'clock on Sunday morning.
2. The competition is at half past twelve.
3. There are sixteen boys and girls in Jerry's team.
4. At quarter past one Jerry has got his first race./
Jerry has got his first race at quarter past one.
5. Tom's race is at quarter to three.
6. It's Tom's fourteenth race.
7. third and ninth

6 (Kapitel 25)
Lösungsvorschlag:
2. Number fifty-six is second.
3. Number twenty-two is third.
4. Number fifteen is fourth.
5. Number nine is fifth.

Wortliste

A

a – ein, eine
about – über
adult – Erwachsene/-r
after – nach
afternoon – Nachmittag
again – noch einmal
airport – Flughafen
all (the) – alle
all day – den ganzen Tag
alone – allein
always – immer
a.m.– vormittags
  6 a.m. – 6 Uhr morgens
  6 p.m. – 6 Uhr abends
an – ein, eine
and – und
animal – Tier
another – noch ein, eine, eins
answer – Antwort
apple – Apfel
are – bist, seid, sind
to arrive – ankommen
arrow – Pfeil
to ask – fragen
at – bei, an, in

B

back – zurück
bag – Schultasche
baggage – Gepäck
ball – Ball
balloon – Ballon
banana – Banane
band – Band, Musikgruppe
bank – Sparkasse
bar – Tafel, Riegel
to bark – bellen
bathroom – Badezimmer
to be – sein
beach – Strand
bed – Bett
bedroom – Schlafzimmer
bee – Biene
before – bevor
behind – hinter
to believe – glauben
bell – Glocke
best – beste/-r/-s
better – besser
big – groß
bike – Fahrrad
birthday – Geburtstag
black – schwarz
to blow up – in die Luft jagen
blue – blau
board – Tafel, Brett
on board – an Bord
boat – Boot
book – Buch
to book – buchen
boring – langweilig
born – geboren
to borrow – ausleihen
both – beide
bottle – Flasche
bow – Bogen
bowl – Schüssel
box – Schachtel, Karton, Kiste
boy – Junge
bread – Brot
to break – brechen
breakfast – Frühstück
bridge – Brücke
to bring – mitbringen, bringen
British – britisch
brochure – Broschüre
brother – Bruder
brown – braun
to brush – bürsten
to build – bauen, aufbauen
burger – Burger
bus (pl. buses) – Bus
bus stop – Bushaltestelle
busy – beschäftigt
but – aber
to buy – kaufen
by – mit
Bye! – Tschüs!

C

cabin – Kajüte, Hütte
cage – Käfig
cafe – Cafe
cafeteria – Cafeteria
cake – Kuchen
call – Anruf
to call – anrufen, rufen, nennen
camera – Kamera
can – können
candle – Kerze
cap – Kappe, Schirmmütze
captain – Kapitän
car – Auto
card – Karte, Spielkarte
caretaker – Hausmeister/- in
carrot – Karotte
to carry – tragen
cat – Katze
to catch – fangen
CD – CD

centre – Mitte, Zentrum
chair – Stuhl
charity – Wohltätigkeitsverein
championship – Wettkampf
to chase – verfolgen, jagen
to cheat – mogeln
to check in – einchecken
to check out – auschecken
cheese – Käse
cherry (pl. cherries) – Kirsche
chicken – Huhn
child – (pl. children) – Kind
chimney – Kamin
chocolate – Schokolade
chorus – Refrain
Christmas – Weihnachten
church – Kirche
cinema – Kino
to clap – klatschen
class – Klasse
classroom – Klassenraum
clean – sauber
to clean – aufräumen, putzen
clever – schlau, klug
clock – Uhr
alarm clock – Wecker
to close – schließen
closed – geschlossen
clothes – Kleidung
club – Club, Verein
coach – Kutsche, Reisebus
coin – Münze
cold – kalt
to collect – sammeln
colour – Farbe
to come – kommen
come down – herunterkommen
comic – Comic
communication – Verständigung, Kommunikation
to compare – vergleichen
competition – Wettkampf
computer – Computer
to connect – verbinden
cook – Koch/ Köchin
to cook – kochen
cool – cool, klasse
to copy – kopieren, abschreiben
corner – Ecke
cornflake – Cornflake
correct – richtig
to correct – korrigieren
cosy – gemütlich
to count – zählen
country – (pl. countries) – Land
cousin – Cousin/Cousine
to cover – bedecken
cow – Kuh
cracker – Knallbonbon
crew – Besatzung
cricket – Kricket
crisp – Kartoffelchip
to cross – überqueren, kreuzen
cupboard – Schrank
curtain – Vorhang
customer – Kunde/Kundin
to cut – schneiden
cute – süß, niedlich

D

dad – Vati, Papa
dance – Tanz
to dance – tanzen
date – Datum
daughter – Tochter
day – Tag
dead – tot
dear – Schatz
Dear… – Liebe(r) …
December – Dezember
deck chair – Liegestuhl
department store – Kaufhaus, Warenhaus
desk – Lehrerpult, Schreibtisch
dessert – Nachtisch
dialogue – Dialog, Gespräch
diary – Tagebuch
dictionary – Wörterbuch
to die – sterben
different – anders, andere
dining-room – Esszimmer
dirty – dreckig
disco – Disko
to dive – tauchen
divorced – geschieden
to do – tun, machen
dog – Hund
to take a dog for a walk – mit dem Hund spazieren gehen
door – Tür
down – entlang, herunter, hinunter, nach unten
downstairs – unten (in einem Gebäude)

Wortliste

drama – Schauspiel
to draw – zeichnen
drawing pin – Reißzwecke
dream – Traum
dress – Kleid
drink – Getränk
to drink – trinken
to drive – fahren
driver – Fahrer/-in
drum – Trommel
to play the drums – Schlagzeug spielen
during – während
dwarf (pl. dwarves) – Zwerg

E

each other – einander
ear – Ohr
east – Osten
Easter – Ostern
easy – einfach, leicht
to eat – essen
egg – Ei
end – Ende
to end – zu Ende gehen, enden, beenden
English – englisch, Englisch
enough – genug
European – Europäer/-in
even – sogar
evening – Abend
event – Veranstaltung
every – jede/-r/-s
everybody – jede/-r/-s
everything – alles
everywhere – überall
example – Beispiel
excited – aufgeregt
exciting – aufregend
Excuse me. – Entschuldigung!, Entschuldige!, Entschuldigen Sie!
exercise – Übung
exercise book – Heft
expensive – teuer
to explain – erklären
extra – extra, besonders
eye – Auge

F

face – Gesicht
fair – Fest, Markt; Jahrmarkt
fairy – Fee
to fall – fallen
false – falsch
family – Familie
famous – berühmt
far – weit
farm – Bauernhof
farmer – Bauer/Bäuerin
fast – schnell
father – Vater
favourite – Lieblings -...
February – Februar
to feed – füttern
to feel – fühlen
ferry (pl. ferries) – Fähre
festival – Festival, Fest
a few – ein paar, einige
field – Wiese, Sportfeld
fight – Streit, Kampf
to fight – kämpfen
to fill in – ausfüllen
film – Film
finally – schließlich
to find – finden
fine – gut
finger – Finger
to finish – beenden, fertig machen
fire – Feuer
first – zuerst, als Erste/-r/-s, erste/-r/-s
fish (pl. fish) – Fisch
flag – Flagge
flat – Wohnung
flour – Mehl
flower – Blume
folder – Hefter, Mappe, Ordner
to follow – folgen
food – Lebensmittel
foot (pl. feet) – Fuß
football – Fußball
for – für
to forget – vergessen
fork – Gabel
form – Form
fox – Fuchs
free – kostenlos, frei
French – französisch, Französisch
Friday – Freitag
on Fridays – freitags
fridge – Kühlschrank
friend – Freund/-in
frog – Frosch
from – von, aus
fruit – Obst
full – voll
fun – Spaß
funny – lustig, komisch
furniture – Möbel

G

game – Spiel
garden – Garten
German – deutsch, Deutsch, Deutsche/-r
to get – bekommen
to get lost – sich verirren
to get to – zu/nach ... kommen
to get up – aufstehen
ghost – Geist
gift shop – Geschenkladen
girl – Mädchen
to give – geben
glass – Glas
to go – gehen
goat – Ziege
gold – Gold
good – gut
goodbye – tschüs, auf Wiedersehen
goose (pl. geese) – Gans
gram – Gramm
grammar – Grammatik
grandad – Opa
grandfather – Großvater
grandma – Oma
grandmother – Großmutter
grandpa – Opa
grandparents – Großeltern
grass – Gras
great – großartig, toll, klasse
Greek – Griechisch, griechisch, Grieche/Griechin
green – grün
grey – grau
grid – Tabelle, Gitter
group – Gruppe, Klasse
to guess – erraten, raten
guide – Führer/-in
guitar – Gitarre
guys – Leute, Jungs

H

half (pl. halves) – Hälfte
half past three – halb vier
hall – Aula, Saal, Flur
ham – Schinken
hand – Hand
to happen – passieren, geschehen
happy – fröhlich, glücklich
hard – hart, fest
hat – Hut
to have – haben
to have got – haben, besitzen
he – er
head – Kopf
heading – Überschrift
headteacher – Schulleiter/-in
to hear – hören
hedgehog – Igel
hello – hallo
help – Hilfe
to help – helfen
her – ihr/ – e, sie, ihr
here – hier
him – ihn, ihm
hip – Hüfte
his – sein/-e
hobby – Hobby
to hold – halten
home – zu Hause
homework – Hausaufgaben
horse – Pferd
hostel – Herberge
youth hostel – Jugendherberge
hot – heiß
hour – Stunde
how – wie
hungry – hungrig
hurry – Eile

I

I – ich
ice cream – Eis
idea – Idee, Einfall, Ahnung
idiot – Idiot/-in
ill – krank
in – in, herein, hinein
to include – beinhalten
information – Information
interested – interessiert
interesting – interessant
Internet – Internet
into – in, hinein
invitation – Einladung
to invite – einladen
irregular – unregelmäßig
is – ist / isn't – ist nicht
island – Insel
it – er, sie, es, ihm, ihn, ihr
Italian – italienisch, Italienisch, Italiener/-in
its – sein/-e, ihr/-e

J

January – Januar
jeans – Jeans

Wortliste

joke – Witz
jolly – fröhlich, vergnügt
juice – Saft
July – Juli
jumbled – durcheinander geworfen
to jump – springen
June – Juni
just – nur

K

key – Schlüssel
kid – Kind
to kill – töten
kin – Verwandte/-r
kind – Art
kiss – Kuss
to kiss – küssen
kitchen – Küche
knife (pl. knives) – Messer
to knock – klopfen
to know – wissen, kennen

L

lamb – Lamm
land – Festland
language – Sprache
lantern – Laterne
large – groß
last – letzte/-r/-s
late – zu spät
later – später
to laugh – lachen
lazy – faul
to learn – lernen
to leave – abfahren, verlassen
left – links, linke/-r/-s; übrig
on the left – links
leg – Bein
lemonade – Limonade
lesson – Unterrichtsstunde
let's – lass/t uns
letter – Brief
library – Bibliothek, Bücherei
to lie – liegen, lügen
life (pl. lives) – Leben
to lift – heben
like – ähnlich, wie
to like – mögen, gern haben
line – Linie
lip – Lippe
list – Liste
to listen – zuhören, (an)hören
listening – Hören, Hörübung
little – klein
to live – leben
living room – Wohnzimmer
long – lang
to look – schauen, sehen, aussehen
to look at – ansehen
a lot – sehr, viel
lots (of) – viel
loud – laut
Love,… – Herzliche Grüße
to love – lieben
You're lucky. – Du hast Glück.
luggage – (Reise)Gepäck
lunch – Mittagessen
lunchtime – Mittagszeit
lying – siehe to lie

M

magazine – Zeitschrift
to make – machen, tun
man (pl. men) – Mann
manager – Geschäftsführer/-in
many – viele
map – Stadtplan, Landkarte
marathon – Marathonlauf
March – März
market – Markt
married – verheiratet
to match – zuordnen
May – Mai
may – dürfen
maybe – vielleicht
me – mich, mir, ich
to mean – bedeuten, meinen
meaning – Bedeutung
medium – mittel
to meet – treffen
menu – Speisekarte
mess – Unordnung, Durcheinander
message – Nachricht
milk – Milch
mind map – Wörternetz
mini – Mini –
minute – Minute
mistake – Fehler
missing – fehlend
to mix – mischen
mobile – Handy
at the moment – im Augenblick
Monday – Montag
money – Geld

month – Monat
more – mehr, weitere
morning – Morgen; Vormittag
mother – Mutter
mouse (pl. mice) – Maus
mouth – Mund, Maul
movie – Film
Mr – Herr
Mrs – Frau
much – viel
mum – Mutti, Mama
museum – Museum
music – Musik
must – müssen
mustn't – nicht dürfen
my – mein/e

N

name – Name
nasty – scheußlich, grässlich
naughty – unartig, ungezogen, frech
near – in der Nähe von, nahe
to need – brauchen
needn't – nicht müssen, nicht brauchen
neighbour – Nachbar/-in
never – nie
new – neu
newsagent – Zeitungsladen
newspaper – Zeitung
next – nächste/-r
next to – neben
nice – schön, nett
night – Nacht
no – nein, kein/-e
nobody – niemand
noise – Geräusch
north – Norden
nose – Nase
not – nicht
November – November
now – nun
number – Zahl, Nummer

O

o'clock – Uhr
October – Oktober
of – von
of course – selbstverständlich
often – oft
old – alt
on – auf, am
only – einzige/-r/-s; nur, erst, bloß
to open – öffnen, aufmachen
opening time – Öffnungszeit
opposite – gegenüber, Gegenteil
or – oder
orange – orange
order – Reihenfolge, Bestellung
to order – bestellen
to organize – organisieren
other – andere/-r/-s
the others – die anderen
our – unser/-e
outside – draußen, nach draußen
over – über, vorbei
over there – da/dort drüben
own – eigen/-e/-er

P

to pack – packen
packet – Päckchen, Packung
page – Seite
to paint – anstreichen, malen
pair – Paar
paper – Papier
parents – Eltern
park – Park
to park – parken
parrot – Papagei
part – Rolle
partner – Partner/-in
party – Feier, Party
past – nach
pen – Füller
pencil – Bleistift
pencil case – Federmäppchen
penny (pl. pence) – Penny, Pence
people – Leute
to perform – ausführen
person (pl. people) – Person
pet – Haustier
phone – Telefon
phone number – Telefonnummer
to phone – anrufen
photo – Foto
phrase – Redewendung, Ausdruck
piano – Klavier
picnic – Picknick
picture – Bild
piece – Stück, Teil
pig – Schwein

Wortliste

pink – rosa, pink
pirate – Pirat/-in
pizza – Pizza
place – Platz, Ort, Stelle
plan – Plan
planner – Jahresplaner
plate – Teller
play – Theaterstück
to play – spielen
playground – Schulhof, Spielplatz
please – bitte
plenty – genug, ausreichend
p.m. – nachmittags
pocket – (Hosen)Tasche
poem – Gedicht
to point – zeigen
police – Polizei
policeman – Polizist
polite – höflich
pond – Teich
pony – Pony
poor – arm
postcard – Postkarte
poster – Poster
pound – Pfund (Gewicht und Währung)
practice – Übung, Probe, Training
to practice – üben
to prepare – vorbereiten
present – Geschenk
to present – präsentieren
presentation – Präsentation
price – Preis (einer Ware)
prize – Preis (den man gewinnt)
problem – Problem
programme – Programm
project – Projekt
to pull – ziehen
pullover – Pullover
pupil – Schüler/-in
purple – lila
to push – stoßen
to put – legen, setzen, stellen
puzzle – Rätsel

Q

quarter – Viertel
quarter to – Viertel vor
quarter past – Viertel nach
question – Frage
quick – schnell (Adjektiv)
quickly – schnell (Adverb)
quiet – ruhig, still
quiz – Quiz, Ratespiel

R

rabbit – Kaninchen
race – Rennen, Lauf
radio – Radio
rain – Regen
to rain – regnen
raincoat – Regenmantel
raisin – Rosine
rap – Rap
rat – Ratte
raven – Rabe
to read – lesen
ready – fertig
real – echt
really – wirklich
recipe – Rezept
red – rot
regular – regelmäßig
reindeer – Rentier
relative – Verwandte/-r
to remember – sich erinnern, denken an, nicht vergessen
to repeat – wiederholen
reporter – Reporter/-in
revision – Wiederholung
rich – reich
ride – Ritt
to ride – reiten, fahren
right – rechts, richtig, rechte/-r/-es
on the right – rechts
right now – jetzt gerade
ring – Ring
to ring – läuten, klingeln
river – Fluss
road – Straße
role – Rolle
room – Raum
round – um ... herum
rubber – Radiergummi
rubbish – Abfall
ruler – Lineal
to run – rennen, laufen
to run away – weglaufen
Russian – russisch, Russisch, Russe/Russin

S

safari – Safari
to sail – segeln
the same – derselbe, dieselbe, dasselbe
sandwich – belegtes Brot
Saturday – Samstag
sausage – Wurst
to say – sagen
scar – Narbe

scared – ängstlich
scary – unheimlich, gruselig
scene – Kulisse, Szene
school – Schule
school bag – Schultasche
scone – brötchenartiges Gepäck
to score a goal – ein Tor schießen
to scream – schreien
sea – Meer
seasick – seekrank
season – Jahreszeit
second – Sekunde, zweite/-r
secret – Geheimnis
to see – sehen, jemanden treffen
to sell – verkaufen
to send – schicken, senden
sentence – Satz
September – September
she – sie
shed – Schuppen
sheep (pl. sheep) – Schaf
ship – Schiff
shoe – Schuh
shop – Geschäft, Laden
shopping – Einkaufen, Einkäufe machen
short – kurz
to shout – schreien
show – Aufführung
to show – zeigen
to shut - schließen
sight – Sehenswürdigkeit
silk – Seide
silly – dumm, albern
to sing – singen
sister – Schwester
to sit – sich setzen, sitzen
situation – Situation
size – Größe
skates – Rollschuhe
skateboard – Skateboard
skill – Fertigkeit, Fähigkeit
skirt – Rock
slave – Sklave
to sleep – schlafen
small – klein
smaller – kleiner
to smile – lächeln
smoke – Rauch
to smoke - rauchen
snack – Snack, Imbiss
snow – Schnee
snowball – Schneeball
Snow White – Schneewittchen
so – also, so, deshalb
sofa – Sofa
some – einige, ein paar, etwas
something – etwas, irgendetwas
sometimes – manchmal
son – Sohn
song – Lied
soon – bald
Sorry. – Entschuldigung.
to sort – sortieren
sound – Geräusch
south – Süden
to speak – sprechen
special – besondere/-s
spell – Zauberspruch, Bann
to spell – buchstabieren
to put a spell on somebody – verzaubern
spooky – gespenstisch
sport – Sport
spring – Frühling, Frühjahr
stage – Bühne
stall – Stand
to stand - stehen
to stand up – aufstehen
to stare – starren
to start – anfangen
to stay – übernachten, bleiben
to steal – stehlen
stepfather – Stiefvater
still – noch, immer noch
stocking – Strumpf
to stop – aufhören, anhalten
stored – gelagert
story – Geschichte
storyteller – Erzähler/-in
straight – gerade
strange – merkwürdig
strawberry – Erdbeere
street – Straße
style – Stil
subject – Unterrichtsfach, Subjekt (Grammatik)
suddenly – plötzlich
sugar – Zucker
suitcase – Koffer
summer – Sommer
sun – Sonne
Sunday – Sonntag
sunglasses (pl.) – Sonnenbrille
sunny – sonnig
super – super, toll
supermarket – Supermarkt
surprise – Überraschung

Wortliste

sweatshirt – Sweatshirt
sweet – Bonbon, süß, niedlich
to swim – schwimmen
to go swimming – schwimmen gehen

T

table – Tisch
tail – Schwanz
to take – nehmen, bringen, dauern
talk – Gespräch, Unterhaltung
to talk – sprechen, reden
taxi – Taxi
tea – Tee
teacher – Lehrer/-in
team – Mannschaft, Team
to tell – sagen, erzählen
tent – Zelt
text – Text
thank you – danke
Thank you very much. – Vielen Dank.
that – das
the – der, die das
theatre – Theater
their – ihr/-e
them – sie/ihnen
then – dann
there – dort, da
these – diese (hier)
they – sie (pl.)
thing – Ding, Sache
to think – denken, glauben
third – dritte/-r/-es
this – das, dies, diese/-r/-es
those – diese (da), die (da), jene
through – durch
to throw – werfen
Thursday – Donnerstag
ticket – Fahrschein, Eintrittskarte
to tidy up – aufräumen
time – Mal, Zeit, Uhrzeit
tiny – winzig
tip – Tipp
tired – müde
title – Titel, Überschrift
to – an, zu, nach
today – heute
together – zusammen, miteinander
tonight – heute Abend, heute Nacht
tomorrow – morgen
too – auch
tooth (pl. teeth) – Zahn
torch – Taschenlampe
tourist – Tourist/-in
towel – Handtuch
town – Stadt
toy – Spielzeug
tractor – Traktor
tradition – Tradition
train – Zug
trainer – Turnschuh
transport – Verkehrsmittel
to travel – reisen
treasure – Schatz
tree – Baum
trip – Ausflug
trouble – Schwierigkeiten
trousers (pl.) – Hose
true – richtig, wahr
to try – versuchen, probieren
Tuesday – Dienstag
tunnel – Tunnel
turkey – Truthahn
Turkish – türkisch, Türkisch
turn – an der Reihe
to turn – abbiegen
tutor – Klassenlehrer/-in
tutor group – Klasse

U

umbrella - (Regen)Schirm
uncle – Onkel
under – unter
underlined – unterstrichen
to understand – verstehen
unhappy – unglücklich
uniform – Uniform
unit – Kapitel
until – bis
up – oben, nach oben, hinauf
upstairs – oben (in einem Gebäude)
us – uns
to use – verwenden
useful – nützlich
usually – gewöhnlich, normalerweise

V

vegetable – Gemüse
very – sehr
vehicle – Fahrzeug
to visit – besuchen
visitor – Besucher/-in
voice – Stimme
volleyball – Volleyball

W

to wait – warten
to wake up – aufwachen
walk – Spaziergang, Wanderung
to walk – gehen, laufen
wall – Mauer, Wand
to want – wollen
wardrobe – Kleiderschrank
warm – warm
was – war
to wash – waschen
watch – Armbanduhr
to watch – (zu)schauen, gucken
Watch out! – Pass auf!, Vorsicht!
water – Wasser
to wave – winken
way – Weg
we – wir
to wear – tragen
weather – Wetter
Wednesday – Mittwoch
week – Woche
weekend – Wochenende
welcome – willkommen
were – waren
west – Westen
wet – nass
what – was
wheel – Rad, Lenkrad
when – wann
where – wo, wohin
which – welche/-r/-s
to whisper – flüstern
to whistle – pfeifen
white – weiß
who – wer, wem, wen
why – wieso
to win – gewinnen
wind – Wind
window – Fenster
windy – windig
winter – Winter
wish – Wunsch
to wish – wünschen
witch – Hexe
with – bei, mit
without – ohne
woman (pl. women) – Frau
wooden – hölzern
the woods - Wald
word – Wort
work – Arbeit
to work – arbeiten, funktionieren
worker – Arbeiter/-in
world – Welt
to write – schreiben
wrong – falsch

Y

year – Jahr, Klasse
yellow – gelb
yes – ja
you – du, ihr, Sie, Ihnen
young – jung
younger – jüngere/-r/-s
your – dein/-e, euer/eure, Ihr/-e
yourselves – selbst

Z

zero – Null

Unregelmäßige Verben

Infinitiv	Simple past	Deutsch
to be	was / were	sein
to become	became	werden
to begin	began	beginnen
to blow	blew	blasen, wehen
to break	broke	(zer)brechen
to bring	brought	bringen
to build	built	bauen
to buy	bought	kaufen
to catch	caught	fangen
to choose	chose	wählen
to come	came	kommen
to cost	cost	kosten
to cut	cut	schneiden
to do	did	tun, machen
to draw	drew	zeichnen, ziehen
to drink	drank	trinken
to drive	drove	fahren
to eat	ate	essen
to fall	fell	fallen
to feed	fed	füttern
to feel	felt	fühlen
to fight	fought	kämpfen
to find	found	finden
to fly	flew	fliegen
to forget	forgot	vergessen
to get	got	bekommen
to give	gave	geben
to go	went	gehen
to have	had	haben
to hear	heard	hören

Unregelmäßige Verben

Infinitiv	Simple past	Deutsch
to hide	hid	verstecken
to hit	hit	treffen / schlagen
to hold	held	halten
to hurt	hurt	verletzen
to know	knew	wissen
to learn	learnt / learned	lernen
to leave	left	verlassen
to let	let	lassen
to make	made	machen
to meet	met	treffen
to put	put	setzen, stellen
to read	read	lesen
to ride	rode	fahren, reiten
to ring	rang	klingeln
to run	ran	rennen
to say	said	sagen
to see	saw	sehen
to sell	sold	verkaufen
to send	sent	senden
to sit	sat	sitzen
to sing	sang	singen
to sleep	slept	schlafen
to speak	spoke	sprechen
to stand	stood	stehen
to swim	swam	schwimmen
to take	took	nehmen
to tell	told	erzählen
to think	thought	denken
to write	wrote	schreiben

Bildnachweis

Seite 18: Pizza: fotolia.de/ Nicholas Piccillo, Salat: fotolia.de/ Robyn Mackenzie, Tennisschläger: PhotoDisc, Inc., Basketball: istockphoto.com/ James McQuillan, Skateboard: Daniel Guffanti, Bus: fotolia.de/ andresr; Katze: istockphoto.com/ Antonio Nunes, Frosch: fotolia.de/ Marcus Jones

Seite 2: Hund: istockphoto.com/ danny zhan, Frau: istockphoto.com/ Daniel St.Pierre, Mädchen: istockphoto.com/ Martin Hendriks, zwei Jungen: istockphoto.com/ Wouter van Caspel

Seite 22: Pizza essen: istockphoto.com/ Galina Barskaya, Tennis spielen: istockphoto.com/ branislav ostojic,
Fahrrad fahren: dreamtime.com/ Godfer, Auto fahren: fotolia.de/ Elenathewise

Seite 25: Junge mit Spielkonsole: fotolia.de/ Tino Hemmann, zwei Jungen: istockphoto.com/ Wendy Shiao

Seite 43: alle Fotos: EKS GmbH, Stuttgart

Seite 52: rechts abbiegen: fotolia.de/ foto.fritz, links abbiegen verboten: istockphoto.com, Eis verboten: istockphoto.com/ christine balderas, Ampel: Tamara Ziegler, Stuttgart, Handy verboten: fotolia.de/ Tina Rencelj

Seite 56: Schweine: istockphoto.com/ Sandy Jones, Ball: istockphoto.com/ simon askham
Katze: istockphoto.com/ Antonio Nunes, Computer: MEV Verlag GmbH, Augsburg
Pferd: istockphoto.com/ Dean Millar, Schultasche: fotolia.de/ Josef Muellek
Kuh: istockphoto.com, Fahrrad: istockphoto.com

Seite 62: Schaf: istockphoto.com, Kuchen: istockphoto.com/ Philip Lange, Keks: istockphoto.com/ Shaun Lowe, Baby: istockphoto.com/ René Jansa, Kirche: David Gaylor, Auge: istockphoto.com/ Cristian Ardelean, Familie: istockphoto.com, Flasche: istockphoto.com/ Tom Werner

Seite 74: links abbiegen verboten: dreamstime.com/ Cyron, sprechen verboten: fotolia.de/ Franck Camhi, schwimmen verboten: dreamstime.com/ Lanceb, Fußball spielen verboten: Jones Ball: istockphoto.com/ simon askham, Helmpflicht: bigstockphoto.com/ phototrekker, Hände waschen: istockphoto.com/ Nuno Silva

Seite 81: Uhren: EKS GmbH, Stuttgart